SOUL
and
SELF

SOUL
and
SELF

Parallels between Spiritual and
Psychological Growth

Paul K. Fehrenbach, PhD

Paulist Press
New York/Mahwah, N.J.

The Publisher gratefully acknowledges use of the following materials:

Reprinted by permission of the publishers and the Trustees of Amherst College from *The Poems of Emily Dickinson*, Thomas H. Johnson, ed., Cambridge, Mass.: The Belknap Press of Harvard University Press, Copyright © 1951, 1955, 1979, 1983 by the President and Fellows of Harvard College.

Poem 7—excerpt of 41.—from *Selected Poems of Rainer Maria Rilke, A Translation from the German and Commentary by Robert Bly*, Copyright © 1981 by Robert Bly. Reprinted by permission of HarperCollins Publishers.

Permission to reprint one line from "All the Way Down" given by New Directions Publishing Corporation, New York City.

Cover design by Sharyn Banks
Book design by Lynn Else

Library of Congress Cataloging-in-Publication Data

Fehrenbach, Paul K.
Soul and self : parallels between spiritual and psychological growth / Paul K. Fehrenbach.
    p. cm.
Includes bibliographical references.
ISBN 0-8091-4423-9 (alk. paper)
1. Catholic men—Psychology—Case studies. 2. Catholic men—Religious life—Case studies. 3. Augustine, Saint, Bishop of Hippo—Psychology. 4. Augustine, Saint, Bishop of Hippo. Confessiones. 5. Developmental psychology—Religious aspects—Catholic church. I. Title.
BX2352.5.F44 2006
282.081—dc22

                                                        2006010352

Published by Paulist Press
997 Macarthur Boulevard
Mahwah, New Jersey 07430

www.paulistpress.com

Printed and bound in the United States of America

CONTENTS

PREFACE

This is a book about psychological and spiritual development in men. It is not a book about becoming more "successful" or even about being a "better person." Rather, it has to do with the questions that lie more at the heart of who we are as men. How can we find and sustain a sense of vitality and meaning in our lives as we mature in a busy world? What roles can we take in our family and also within the larger community that will allow us to contribute to the welfare of others while remaining attentive to our own personal growth?

I believe that healthy psychological and spiritual development cooperate with each other. Psychological growth promotes spiritual development, and spiritual growth enriches psychological life. It is best not to make artificial separations between these two dimensions of human living, however, since the psychological and spiritual aspects of the human journey are not antithetical but complementary to each other.

At the core of human development lies what some psychologists call the "self" and spiritual writers refer to as the "soul." Both psychology and religion see this center as a rich source of guidance and renewal for our lives. This book is concerned with how to identify and attend to the voice of the soul as it manifests itself in different contexts along the entire life span. Each developmental era offers opportunities for recognizing the presence of the soul. For many men, the midlife period of development seems to provide special circumstances that stimulate the reflective attitude necessary for this process to begin. If we follow the path enlightened by this inner guide, we are more likely to anticipate conflicts and recognize opportunities for living a life that is both faithful to ourselves as well as helpful to others.

My primary model for describing the psychological dimension of healthy development is a man I am calling "Charlie." Charlie was about forty-two years old when he first came in to see me. We were involved in psychotherapy together for several years. During that time, he faced some problems shared by many men during the midlife period of development. Though he resolved them in his own unique ways, the steps that he took provide the rest of us with a practical example of how to rectify our mistakes and create a more meaningful life. Charlie shows us how a man can learn to hear the voice of his soul and find rich opportunities to mature during his middle years.

My primary model for describing the spiritual dimension of this process is taken from the life of a man named Augustine. He was a Catholic bishop who lived in the North African region currently known as Algeria during the years 354 to 430. When he was forty-three years old, he wrote a book that he called his *Confessions*. It was one of the first autobiographies ever written and remains a time-honored classic.

My introduction to Augustine came in 1966, when I was a newly arrived Peace Corps volunteer in a small village in Algeria's neighbor, Tunisia. At that time, the Peace Corps provided volunteers in remote locations with a three-foot-high cardboard box called a "book locker." When you swung open this container, it became a ready-made bookcase with about one hundred paperbacks neatly stacked on six built-in shelves. What's more, each book was arranged in alphabetical order. On the far left of the top shelf was Augustine's *Confessions,* and on the far right of the bottom shelf was a novel by the French writer Émile Zola. The simple order of this little box had a special appeal to me as I started adjusting to my confusing new hometown. Since I was going to be living in that same place for the next two years, I decided to begin with the letter *A* and work my way through the collection. That's how I first became acquainted with Augustine.

As I started reading the *Confessions,* I was also beginning my assigned job as a teacher in the local school. The boys and girls in my classes were the first generation to sit in those rows of desks. They were eager and enthusiastic students who seemed to view any confinement to classroom furniture as an impediment to their learning. The Augustine I was meeting in the *Confessions* grew up in the same kind of school, in a village just like mine, that was not so far away. As he described his boyhood days in school, I could easily imagine him as the kind of playful, mischievous student that I encountered each day in my own classroom.

Later on in the book, when Augustine grew up and became a high school teacher himself, I could identify with him as a colleague. As he described growing older and struggling with spiritual issues, I was amazed at how clearly he posed questions that I was facing in my own life. During the past forty years, I have continued to read the *Confessions.* Despite the centuries that separate our lifetimes, what he had to say has remained very helpful to me. I am passing along some of my own reflections on the parallels between psychological and spiritual development that have grown out of a lifetime dialogue with this man.

The person who inspired the psychological framework for this book was someone I met in September 1972. I had just completed my PhD and was beginning my first job as a clinical psychologist in a mental health center located in Durham, North Carolina. In the office next to mine, also newly arrived, was a psychiatrist named Kathleen Stewart. Kathleen was in the final years of a long and distinguished career spent mostly in California with one of the respected pillars of our profession, Erik Erikson. She had come to this small mental health center to give two years of her work life to what she liked to call her "Peace Corps Service." Despite our differences in age and experience, which may have totaled forty years, we soon discovered how much we also had in common. I spent many hours with Kathleen, watching her work and learning what I could from her vast reservoir of clinical knowledge and wisdom. She was not only my teacher, but my dear friend until she died in 1975.

Kathleen spoke often of the deep admiration she felt for her own teacher, Erik Erikson. She enjoyed telling me stories about the experiences and ideas they had shared over the years. One day she told me that, of the recognitions she had been privileged to receive during her professional career, she was most honored to be mentioned by Erikson in a footnote cited on page 198 in his book *Insight and Responsibility*. In the text above that footnote, Erikson had been describing Freud's classic notion of the "censor" and how it operated within the psyche to prevent or revise undesirable memories and feelings as they emerged into consciousness. He then cited Kathleen's suggestion that if there were a "censor," then there might be a "sponsor" as well. If a censor could inhibit, then a sponsor might function to promote the emergence of life in the inner world.

Kathleen Stewart's notion of the importance of a sponsor for psychological growth has stuck with me throughout my career. I have come to believe that each of us relies on the facilitating presence of sponsors in our life. Sponsors, like censors, first appear in the external world in the form of specific people we meet. These individuals subsequently are taken into our internal world through the repetition of our experiences or remembrances of them. They are preserved there in our memories, supporting and facilitating our future growth.

I first noticed this with Kathleen herself. As I observed her work with clients, I recognized how she was capable of drawing out such a wide range of previously inhibited memories and feelings simply by her quiet and accepting presence. She was the very embodiment of what she herself would have called a sponsor, that is, a catalyst whose own inner vitality touched and promoted the emergence of life in others. I also could feel the effect of her quiet sponsorship in my own life. Indeed, much of my identity as a young psychologist began to emerge in the compassionate presence of Kathleen Stewart. She has remained with me throughout my long career.

I have been listening to men and women describe their lives to me in psychotherapy for more than thirty years. Some of them report such a sense of vitality and meaning while others experience being "bogged down" or "burned out" with what they are doing and even who they are. One group cannot be distinguished from the other based on external markers like education, income, or list of accomplishments. Over time I have come to see that this is because the locus for evaluating one's life shifts during the middle years. It gradually moves from using outside measures of achievement toward a more internal point of reference. One's personal sense of vitality and meaning becomes increasingly dependent on attention to the inner voice of one's soul.

The focus of this book is on how men can learn to recognize the presence of their soul. I will trace this process through a series of stages. The advantage of describing growth through stages is that it divides something very complex into a series of smaller parts. This approach has its benefits, but also creates a potential problem. Stage theories can give the false impression that life is orderly and progresses in predictable ways. In reality, the path of human development is neither linear nor is growth ever permanently sustained. On any given day, we may be at any given stage, and sustaining our progress takes constant effort. Taking this into account helps us better appreciate the limited but useful role of stages in understanding the complex process of human development.

The following are some ideas I believe are central to the promotion of healthy adult psychological and spiritual growth. To begin with, it is most helpful to focus our attention on the interior life of the "self" or "soul," which shares the common interest of both psychology and religion. It is the soul that will provide us with the guidance we need to give meaning and direction to our life. Identifying its presence is made easier if we start by recognizing the specific people who have been its sponsors and censors over the course of our past history. Healthy psycho-spiritual development can be marked by how well we have learned to nourish that life force in ourselves and others, so that we might pass on the vital heritage of our own sponsorship to each person who now depends on our care. We will begin exploring how this process takes shape by examining the ways that development unfolds during the middle years of a man's life.

INTRODUCTION:
We Encounter the Soul
When We Slow Down
and Listen

S everal years ago a forty-two-year-old man came to see me for psychotherapy. Charlie was a successful owner of a small business who described a long history of unhappiness with his work. More recently, he had experienced a series of significant losses. Two years ago, his father had died after a three-year bout with cancer. Earlier this year, the woman whom he had been planning to marry told him she was no longer interested in continuing the relationship. Susan said she was tired of his work habits and his emotional unavailability.

Charlie was stunned by what seemed to be one more step in the gradual collapse of his personal world. He had lost his first marriage because of these same issues. His father's death had left him with a well of sorrow that still brought him to the point of despair. When Susan withdrew from the relationship, he described his emotional state as one of a "broken heart."

What's more, Charlie no longer felt that he had his work to fall back on. Despite his success, he had been feeling even less satisfaction tending to the day-to-day details of managing the store. While in college he had found himself drawn to be a high school English teacher, but finally gave in to the pressures from his father to take over the family business in retail food. What had given Charlie some level of meaning and satisfaction over the years had been the time spent with his father at the store and the money he made that supported a very comfortable life for his family. His divorce and the death of his father had taken away the main reasons for doing this. Susan's departure dashed the hopes for beginning anew. Charlie not only was left in a state of grief about his past but growing confusion about his future. He felt that he stood at a crossroads in his life.

From the point of view of psychology, Charlie's current pain and confusion might be better understood if viewed from a wider perspective that dates to earlier times in his life. As this man explored the grief he felt for losses extending back to his divorce, he began to recognize a previous loss he had never quite acknowledged. In retrospect, he felt that he had begun to lose his way when he abandoned his dreams to become a teacher for reasons that had more to do with family pressures and less with his heart's desires. Later, after he married Joyce and they had two sons, he built both his marriage and family life on what amounted to a false premise, namely, that he should arrange his daily routine solely around taking care of them financially rather than also focusing on the time he could spend with them in relationship.

When the struggles that Charlie is currently facing are seen in the context of his entire adult life span, they are consistent with patterns that contemporary psychologists associate with the midlife period of male development. Examining these issues from this developmental perspective may help us see some experiences we may have in common with Charlie and perhaps prompt us to face some of these same challenges in our own lives.

Let's look first at the timing. The fact that Charlie experienced these problems in his forties does not automatically qualify them as midlife issues. Chronological age, taken in itself, is an inadequate indicator of a midlife transition. The midlife process falls under the broad definition of a developmental occurrence because it does happen roughly within a given age range. In American culture, for example, most men who identify midlife transitions report going through them sometime between their late thirties and early sixties. The obvious problem, however, with such a wide time span is that it makes recognizing the occurrence of any particular individual's midlife transition a very difficult task if age is used as the sole indicator.

The identification of midlife transitions is further complicated by the popular misconception that the process invariably entails some kind of a "crisis." In fact, *midlife crisis* has become a common phrase used to describe most any turmoil experienced during this period. This error adds to the confusion because it leads some men to downgrade the importance of what they are actually going through because they cannot identify anything about their experience that is dramatic enough to qualify it as a crisis. Others mistakenly assume that some pivotal event that did happen during this period must have been their personal midlife crisis simply because it occurred at that time. Even a crisis that happens during the middle years is not synonymous with a midlife developmental transition. To assume this and then dismiss the more subtle manifestations of the actual experience can deprive some men of benefiting from a potentially rich process in their development.

Having said this, it is also important to examine why this popular linkage of *midlife* and *crisis* may have occurred in the first place. Perhaps one reason is because this developmental transition is sometimes precipitated by a crucial event. During these middle years, many men are confronted with a major life challenge, such as the loss of a marriage or job, a serious illness, a child leaving home, or the death of a parent. The first reaction to such important life events is usually to make whatever adjustments that appear necessary. However, when it comes to dealing with the losses in life as significant as one's family or health or livelihood, there is only so much that can be "solved" simply by making some practical accommodations in the wake of a crisis.

Sooner or later, after life has restabilized, many men go through a second phase of adaptation that is much less visible. They find themselves drawn inward, to a psychological world inside themselves that is neither practical nor rational nor even necessarily hospitable. As the poet Emily Dickinson said, "After great pain a formal feeling comes." This "formal feeling" is the next step in the emotional "drawing inward" that was precipitated by the original stressful event. In this way, the crisis itself is not synonymous with the midlife developmental process, but it is usually the forerunner to it. The actual midlife transition begins during this second, inward phase.

At its core, the midlife transition is an internal process, and therefore it best can be identified by paying attention to what is happening in the inner world of the person who is going through it. It can be understood as a state of mind with certain unique features. First of all, at some point in the middle years, it becomes increasingly clear that there will be very finite limits to whatever one might have hoped to achieve in the course of one's life. Secondly, there is a new awareness of time that includes some personal acknowledgment of death. This awareness of death may be directly connected with a painful event, especially if it involves a loss such as an illness, declining function, or the death of someone personally important. However, it also may be prompted by the occurrence of a decade birthday such as turning forty, fifty, or sixty years old. Whatever the precipitant, many men describe a mental transition from viewing their life in terms of years lived to a new perspective that focuses more on the number of years that remain.

Both of these features—recognition of limits to achievement and personal awareness of death—combine to raise questions about the meaning and purpose of whatever time might remain. These questions are what lie behind the next step in the familiar process that usually shows up at some point during the middle years: the task of reviewing and "taking stock" of one's life and how it has been led so far. This is not necessarily an unpleasant experience or even one that is systematic or detailed. Whatever the extent of the process, most men end up feeling confirmed that their life has taken a reasonably satisfying course over the years and that they are content. Others may opt to proceed on the same path, making only slight modifications. A much smaller number of men, however, draw the conclusion that they will need to make some extensive changes in their work or marital situation, and that there is a dwindling amount of time remaining to do so. Those men who do reach such challenging conclusions are often the ones who report the levels of depression or anxiety that we associate with that popular term *midlife crisis.*

The age of onset for a midlife transition was as unpredictable for Charlie as it is for most men. His age as well as the timing of his most recent painful loss were certainly important external markers. However, these were not enough in themselves. The key additional element had to do with his state of mind. As he spent more time exploring the overview of his life thus far, he reached the painful conclusion that he had been on the wrong path in both his work and love life. Furthermore, if he chose to make any change of course, there was a limited amount of time remaining to make the necessary corrections.

If Charlie had entered therapy even ten years earlier, he probably would have approached his situation from a different perspective. Very likely, there would have been more focus on the recording and ordering of external events. His primary interest at midlife, however, was much more centered on his inner responses to those outer events. He was trying to understand what those experiences meant to him. Consequently, he was less preoccupied with how he might create a more successful and lucrative career in the years ahead. He was also less inclined to continue approaching his life as if it were nothing but a series of problems to be solved and ambitions to be fulfilled.

Charlie's new attitude began to emerge later in therapy as he started to conceive of his entire life in terms of its being a "journey" that was composed of experiences to be understood. This new perspective led him to ask himself a very different set of questions that had more to do with the meaning and purpose of his personal history. The issues that subsequently were raised had not bothered him in such a compelling way since he was an adolescent. Indeed, questions about identity and direction in life that are examined by many men at midlife have to do with the unfinished business of their adolescence and early adult years.

As he proceeded on this inward journey, Charlie found himself drawn forward by something that appeared to lie at the bottom of all this seeming chaos and to offer a possibility of hope. He experienced it as something woven within all the confusion and grief, yet extending even beyond the distress and offering a potential for healing.

Charlie's next step was an important transition in the exploration of his inner world. He reached a key psychological insight that would lie at the foundation of all that was to follow. What he did was to identify and name something he experienced as a kind of center within himself; a point of reference around which he might begin organizing his internal chaos. This center was more than an impersonal anchor. He described it as a living presence within his psyche that was capable of providing him with the strength and guidance he would need to proceed further in this confusing process. Charlie eventually gave a name to this common human experience of a vital source of renewal that exists within the mind. The name he chose came from his earlier religious upbringing as a Catholic. He called this core presence within him his "soul."

The First Step on Our Inner Journey: Recognition of the Soul

Some contemporary psychologists have used the term *self* to describe our common human experience of having a unique center within us which we identify as being our true "me." We experience this self as the vital core of our inner world. It allows us to understand that we are more than our behaviors; that we don't just *do* life, we *experience* it. The self also gives us our sense of coherence and integration over time. Thus, we believe that despite so many outward changes, "I am the same person I was as a child." This vital core can provide us with a sense of understanding and vision for our future. The self gives "plot" to our life; it is capable of endowing past events with meaning and future possibilities with purpose. It goes about this work of meaning and vision making with a language charged with affect and frequently composed of images. The self is the author of our feelings, fantasies, dreams, and hopes. It is the seat of our subjectivity, the center of our initiative, and the source of our creative presence in the world. Above all, the self is generative; it renews and enriches our sense of being alive.

People engaged in psychotherapy often come to refer to having a sense of their own dynamic inner core by some familiar name. They call it "my self," "my soul," "my heart," "my innermost being," "my true self," "my center," "who I truly am," "the real me." One man described his first step in recognizing the presence of his self as identifying his "bubble." He was referring to the circle drawn over the heads of cartoon characters that contains their uncensored opinions and what they truly feel.

In his *Confessions,* Augustine referred to his self as his "soul" and sometimes his "heart." It is important to note that he wrote this autobiography in his early forties. Like Charlie, he was not only grieving painful losses in his personal life, but also sorting out what he wanted to do about work in his future. The specific issues he encountered as well as the manner in which he approached them were all consistent with patterns that contemporary psychologists would associate with a midlife transition. He too found this as an occasion that led to an encounter with his own soul.

The *Confessions* also documents how Augustine first came to distinguish the unique voice of his soul within the larger inner world of his psyche. He did this primarily by slowing down his pace and creating moments of quiet within his busy routine. Like so many people before and after him, he then began to experience his soul as a comforting resource for healing his emotional wounds and a powerful force for renewal in his life.

We Can Hear the Voice of Our Soul If We Slow Down and Listen

Whether at midlife or any point on the developmental continuum, the first step on the modern path of recognizing the voice of the soul involves slowing down and listening. As Walt Whitman said, "I loaf and invite my soul." It is unfortunate that this sense of taking a meaningful pause from activity—"loafing"— is not highly valued in our fast-paced American culture. Many men have been taught from their earliest years not to slow down and listen, but to approach their life as if it were a constant project to be undertaken with efficiency and completed with dispatch. In our culture, a successful life is typically associated with productivity, accomplishment, and wealth. Consequently, too many men arrive at their early adult years already discouraged from following the natural rhythms that they originally felt were present in their lives as young children. They no longer trust the alternating flow of their energy, with its inborn movement from mastery to mystery and back again.

Augustine's book the *Confessions* is first of all a visible representation of his own process of slowing down and listening. The act of writing in itself served as a way of reducing his outer activities and promoting an attitude of reflection on his inner world. There is an old saying in North Africa that may have existed even in Augustine's time, that "a man's soul can travel only as fast as a camel can walk." Writing was his way to slow himself down to a camel's pace so that he might listen to what was going on in his soul. Augustine considered this to be his first insight: "I must plan my time and arrange my day for the good of my soul."

If we wish to hear the voice of our own soul, we too must plan some time to listen. For some of us that may take the form of writing, perhaps in a journal. For others, it could involve walking in a quiet place. Some men pray or meditate. Others prefer to draw, paint, or sculpt. Many simply close the door at home or work for five or ten minutes each day in order to stare out the window as they invite their thoughts and feelings to arise. I know one man who says that his best time for reflection occurs when he is fishing; his hope is that he can pass on his love for that process to his young daughter. Whatever medium and time we prefer, it is important to choose a routine that is comfortable enough to sustain.

Journals, walks, artistic materials, and quiet rooms are the outer manifestations of an inner place and pause that are necessary for access to the inner world. We know we have found the particular form that fits us personally when everything stops except the soul. It is like discovering a favorite bench on a mountain trail where we can safely pause and enjoy the view. Returning regularly to this familiar outer place begins to draw us into an inner space. The poet Gerard Manley Hopkins said that if we look at something long enough it begins to look back at us. Outer perspective becomes inner perspective. It is here that we encounter the soul, not the object but the subject of our journey.

Charlie and Augustine were like many men who end up being dragged, not drawn, into their inner world. It took a series of setbacks to stop both of them in their tracks and force a slowdown to a soul's pace. When each man faced himself in the mirror of self-scrutiny at the middle point of his life, he began to see how far he had strayed from his own path. Fortunately, middle age still provides ample time for review and revision of one's life direction.

In the following chapters we will examine, in practical ways, how that review can take place and the helpful new directions that it may prompt some men to follow.

One

Attending to Our Inner Life: A Skill That Can Be Learned

The journey toward spiritual and psychological health begins when we establish a practice of setting aside time for honestly observing our life. The next step involves learning the skills that assist in that process. Both religion and psychology have long histories of encouraging people to take a pause from their busy routines for engaging in this kind of reflection. In addition, each has also developed a variety of methods for teaching the skills that facilitate productive self-observation.

Practices to promote reflectivity have evolved over centuries in the traditions of Christianity, Islam, Buddhism, and Hinduism. Each has a long-established custom of encouraging participation in days of recollection and retreats designed to promote discernment of the inner life. In addition, religious groups have also given us detailed instructions for how to go about the discernment process. For example, Jesuits have developed a program called the "Ignatian Method." Benedictines teach another step-by-step process they have named "lectio divina." The current popularity of "centering prayer" is similar to some Buddhist and Hindu meditation practices. Christianity, Buddhism, and Islam have also promoted walking styles of meditation. An ambulatory version used by Christians involves reflectively following a path through a labyrinth.

In the Buddhist tradition, there is a wonderful image that describes the challenge faced by anyone trying to see himself more clearly. Buddhists liken self-observation to looking into a mirror. At first we can see our image, but as we look more closely we begin to notice that there is also some dust on the mirror. This dust distorts and clouds our view. Developing the skill to see ourselves ever more clearly requires noticing that dust, and learning the best ways to clean it off the mirror.

The importance of establishing a habit of stepping back to examine our lives is a theme that also runs through the history of contemporary psychology. Learning the process of self-observation is the initial task required in many forms of psychotherapy. Harry Stack Sullivan, an esteemed early contributor to American psychoanalysis, wrote frequently of the significance of becoming a "participant-observer" in our day-to-day living. Healthy psychological functioning, from Sullivan's perspective, means practicing self-observation so habitually that it doesn't just happen at set intervals but becomes a more consistent process that is going on throughout our waking hours. Thus, we not only engage in our daily activities, but we also become a witness to our experience.

The importance of setting aside time for the practice of this self-reflection is sometimes described to clients by their therapists at the outset of psychotherapy. When I finished my initial interview with Charlie I advised him, as I do all my clients, to prepare for his therapy sessions with me by reserving at least a few minutes every day to pay attention to what is going on inside himself. I encouraged him to find a comfortable place to be alone. I recommended that he adopt whatever practice he most enjoys that will facilitate his maintaining these contemplative moments over time. Write in a journal, walk, pray, or simply close the door and put your feet up. Do whatever you want that will fit into your life well enough to make this into a habit.

Furthermore, I asked him to focus his time of self-reflection around one simple question: "What am I finding myself thinking about and feeling today?" Attention should be paid to whatever is spontaneously arising in his mind in the form of preoccupations, fantasies, daydreams, hopes, dreads, or random reactions to events. During this time-out period, he can take the burden off his shoulders of solving his problems and fixing his life. Instead, he can simply pay attention to anything at all that comes to his mind, trying to do so without expectations or criticism of whatever thoughts and feelings that may arise. Our first task is to learn how to listen to ourselves and benefit from our experiences, because we cannot change what we don't understand.

I told him that on the days he comes to his therapy hour with me I would begin each session with the same question: "What have you been thinking about and feeling?" I wanted Charlie to see this office and the time with me as a place of retreat. I reassured him it would be quiet, uninterrupted, focused on his process, and safe from criticism. In my experience, more satisfying solutions to problems and new directions for living become apparent when we learn how to be an honest witness to our own life and develop a sense of trust in the healthy resources for guidance that lie deep within ourselves.

Psychology has a lot to offer to anyone wanting to learn how to become not only a healthy participant but also a compassionate observer of their life. After we have begun to set aside the time and made a habit of paying attention to what we are thinking and feeling, the next steps involve improving the quality of the internal witness. As we shall see, self-observation is essentially a skill. Anyone can learn it, and anyone can learn how to do it better. There are some pitfalls to be avoided and stages in skill acquisition that can be recognized and improved upon. Conscientious engagement in this process has the further benefit of eventually leading many people to a clearer awareness of their self or soul, which is the common ground of psychological and spiritual development.

In the next section, we will look at one description of the various stages in that process of self-awareness that is based on ideas developed by the American psychologist Carl Rogers.

The First Two Stages of Self-Awareness: Trapped in Our Outer World

When we enter the inner world, we need a new set of reference points that are different from the ones we use to trace our external activities. The following stages of psychological processing are based on the work of Carl Rogers as he described them in his book *On Becoming a Person*. They have been modified to fit my own experiences with clients and to suit our purposes here. It should be said at the outset that we do not go through these stages one at a time in a linear progression. The process is much more like a circle that we negotiate repeatedly. Each description of a stage is like a road marker that alerts us to where we are in the overall progression at any given time.

Rogers said that it is common for people to encounter guilt when they first start to reflect on their life. He laid out a series of stages that often take place both before and after that guilt emerges. He believed that these stages consist of a progressive movement from assuming that events take place only in the outer world, to an increasing sense of awareness that there is a corresponding inner world of feelings and dreams. Further steps involve a willingness to give value to that inner world and to trust it as a guide for one's life. He placed hyperawareness of guilt at the third stage of that continuum.

For some people, the sound of guilty self-accusation may be the first consistent voice they hear as they make their initial shift of attention from the outer to the inner dimension of their life. Unless one understands what this is about, it would be easy to become discouraged from going any further. Let's begin by briefly exploring the two stages that sometimes precede this painful awareness of guilt. These two stages might be called "prereflective." They describe a state of mind that exists before an ongoing process of psychological reflection has begun.

The first stage in Rogers's seven levels of psychological awareness is truly prereflective because it describes a way of living in which there is only minimal consciousness of an inner subjective state. Life is lived "out there" in the external world of tasks and details and is focused on mastering the responsibilities of day-to-day living. Feelings and dreams may be recognized, but they are seen as unimportant or unconnected to the challenges of the "real world."

Persons functioning at stage one ignore their subjectivity, which is often evidenced in a denial of having personal problems. If something goes wrong for them they may try to remedy the situation, but these attempts are commonly undertaken without admission of personal culpability. These individuals might actually function quite well at their work, but often show problems sustaining emotionally close relationships with others.

Early on in his therapy, Charlie was already beginning to see how some of these stage-one characteristics had been operating during his first marriage. At the point where his adult life began to unravel with the separation from Joyce, Charlie was surprised to hear her claims that he was "more married to his work than his wife." He had long maintained that his work hours needn't be seen as such a big problem; the main reason he put in so much time was to provide a better life for her and the kids. Unfortunately, this habit of ignoring her pleas for more time together had left him unaware of their growing emotional distance. It had also left the two of them at a place where there was little room to forge some creative compromises that earlier might have sustained the marriage.

After Joyce eventually left him, Charlie protected himself with the attitude, "Things are going just fine; I can handle this." He poured himself even more thoroughly into his work at the store and faithfully carried out his "duty" of looking after their two sons every other weekend. About eight months later, he also started dating. He looked to all the world like a man who had successfully made the transition, but he was following the path too often seen by therapists; that many postdivorce men are more likely to replace a failed relationship than grieve it. At stage one, there is a reluctance to admitting there may be a problem. When we pay so little attention to what is happening in our daily life, it is hard to benefit from our experiences. We are vulnerable to simply repeating what we did before.

This leads us to the second stage, which is closely related to the first. In the second level of self-awareness, personal conflicts and feelings may be more frequently acknowledged, but the causes for them are usually attributed to sources external to the self. When there is an admission of a problem, it is often followed by an attribution of blame: "Yes, I do have marital problems, but they are caused by my wife." "I may have some difficulties at work, but this is because my supervisor is so incompetent." The potential for resolving any of these problems, therefore, depends on changes being made by some other person. In stage two, there is still little sense of responsibility for the creation or the solution of one's interpersonal problems. There is no recognition that we ourselves may be contributing to our conflicts with others; problems are located outside the range of our personal accountability and placed on the shoulders of some other person.

Charlie later voiced some of these stage-two characteristics in his assumptions about Joyce. He believed that the marital problems they were experiencing were the result of her shortcomings. In his mind, she did not accurately understand the demands of the "real world" and that she also didn't appreciate the loving motivations behind his work habits. To whatever degree these attributions were correct, they functioned to keep Charlie from facing his own responsibilities in the breakup of his marriage. Sadly, his avoidance of taking the time he needed to step back and learn from the experience of that first failed relationship now left him facing similar problems with Susan.

Many men who look at the broad sweep of their lives find that they have developed a consistent pattern of externalizing almost everything. Each progressive challenge faced in the normal course of development is converted into an external task to be mastered. From this point of view, almost any experience can be translated into a goal to be accomplished, a problem to be solved, or a hurdle to be overcome. Directions in life then become envisioned in terms of material success and social performance.

When this external approach is followed and setbacks or failures occur, there is a natural tendency to react with blame. If there is a problem, then someone must be at fault. For some men, that blame mainly is focused externally, onto family, co-workers, or people in authority who must have let them down. For others, the blame is experienced internally, leaving some men facing a harsh inner critic ready to scold them for a litany of perceived faults.

The Third Stage of Self-Awareness: Encounters with the Inner Critic

The movement to the third stage of self-observation is characterized by the encounter with a personal critic. At stage three, experiences are processed in a psychological courtroom in front of an internal judge. Each behavior, feeling, thought, or desire is examined in terms of whether it is good or bad, right or wrong, moral or immoral. The language of this inner arbiter is frequently sprinkled with words such as *guilty* or *innocent, should* or *shouldn't, ought to* or *ought not*. In fact, stage-three processing can often be recognized simply by noticing the presence of these key words.

Like Carl Rogers, other psychologists also have distinguished the presence of this distinct voice of judgment that exists in the psyche. Erik Erikson borrowed the term *censor* from Freud. Freud used this term to describe one of the functions of the *superego*. Others have used a variety of rough synonyms for Freud's original superego such as *conscience, should system,* or *inner parent,* to name a few. They have all noted its first appearance very early in life and how its original rules and the relative harshness of its attitude appear to be learned in a social context. The rules and attitude of the internal judge reflect the perceived values of the family and community in which the child was raised.

In the course of his therapy, Charlie gradually began to distinguish the unique voice of his conscience within the larger chaos of his internal world. He came face-to-face with a harsh arbitrator that had been operating just out of sight. Like most "should systems," it had a major theme. Charlie's inner judge measured his personal worth on the basis of the number of hours he worked. He saw how he had spent many years trying to meet what he perceived to be the expectations of his work-focused father as well as please his own inner timekeeper. The effort it took to meet this demanding personal agenda had left his life unbalanced and distracted him from attending to the well-being of his marriage and family.

Charlie's behavior was less the product of malicious intent and more the result of poor choices resulting from an absence of self-reflection. As he slowed down in therapy and encountered these unexamined basic assumptions about how he should act, he saw that he had essentially treated his family in the same way he had treated himself—in a style characterized by neglect.

This was one of the hardest times in Charlie's therapy. He was overcome by guilt. However, this time the guilt was not tied to the time clock. It was associated with the violation of values to which he truly wanted to hold himself accountable: He had let down his wife, his children, and himself. Facing his own responsibility for what happened as well as the consequences of his inaction was the only way that he could hope for any measure of reconciliation with those he had hurt, as well as learn enough from this experience to lessen the chances of repeating it.

The American psychiatrist, Karl Menninger, in his book *Whatever Became of Sin?*, explored the concept of "sin" from this same psychological perspective. Menninger believed that a healthy adult conscience operates as an inner representative of the collective welfare. His sense of sin meant the violation of the well-being of another person in order to achieve one's individual goals. He specifically cited the similarities between his views and the principles Augustine eventually adopted for himself. From Menninger's point of view, both he and Augustine would define sinful behavior as the willful disregard of the welfare of another person in order to pursue one's private agenda. Augustine referred to it in his *Confessions* as a "turning away from the whole to the individual part."

From a spiritual standpoint, the identification of the inner critic has an added dimension of importance. Augustine described the benefit he experienced in distinguishing the presence of his conscience within the larger framework of his inner world. It allowed him to hear it as a separate entity that spoke with a voice that was quite distinct from the other sounds in his psyche. This important insight helped him to recognize how both his psychological and spiritual development were excessively organized around the set point of his conscience, which too often assumed the central position of authority in his psyche.

If the conscience becomes the most powerful inner voice, then psychological development becomes equated with self-improvement, and spiritual growth is relegated to moral rectitude. As we shall see, we must respect the voice of the conscience, but it cannot be allowed to occupy the central position of authority in the psyche if healthy growth and development are going to continue taking place.

In summary, the process of psycho-spiritual development begins to unfold when we find at least a few moments each day to go on our own version of a retreat. We choose a place where we can loaf and invite our soul. When the room is quiet, we ask ourselves some version of the question: "What am I thinking about and feeling?" This is the stimulus that alerts us to step out of the external realm of "doing" and enter the inner world of "being," where we can invite and observe our soul.

At some point in this process, we will surely hear the judgments and censure voiced by an inner "critic," which may actually be quite a powerful presence functioning in our mind. The critic sees everything in terms of moral issues. Its presence can be identified by its language of *right* or *wrong* and *good* or *bad*. Though such judgments are helpful when applied to external behavior, the soul finds more freedom to emerge in an environment free from criticism.

In the next chapter, we will explore another way of paying attention to the internal world. By developing an ability to observe without judgment, we can foster a progression of stages that eventually leads to the emergence of the soul. The self or soul is the crucible where the generative forces of renewal originate in both the psychological and spiritual dimensions. Nonjudgmental observation is an important tool that is necessary to facilitate the unfolding of this process.

Two

Developing the Process of Nonjudgmental Reflection

The first two stages of psychological processing are called pre-reflective, because there is no time given to self-observation, and attention is focused on the outer world. This results in little recognition of inner agency, and hence no sense of personal accountability. Everything can be explained by or blamed on external circumstances. If problems arise, there is a reflexive belief they were caused by someone else. Likewise, solutions are sought from changes originating in some other person.

Stage three is the transition zone from the outer to the inner world and thus from prereflective to reflective processing. This transition is marked by a growing understanding that we are personally responsible for how we react to external events, whether or not we ourselves caused them to happen. Healthy functioning in the third stage sometimes requires the reexamination of the rights and wrongs we learned as children so that we can amend them to reasonable standards that fit the work and relationship responsibilities of an adult. When discrepancies are noticed between these values and behavior, as was the case with Charlie, the full expression of stage-three processing entails facing the guilt that arises and finding ways to reconcile the differences.

We will now examine stages four and five, which constitute the shift from prereflective to reflective processing. The movement from our relationship with the external world, which is the focus of the third stage, to our relationship with the internal world of self-reflection requires making an important mental transition. The conscience occupied the central observational position in the third stage because its evaluations and judgments were necessary for assessing how well we were living up to our responsibilities to others. However, observation of the inner dimension of feelings and desires, which are the focus of the reflective stages, works better if we take a position of suspending those evaluations and judgments. As long as the conscience holds sway, whatever disagrees with its rules will be judged as wrong. That atmosphere leaves too little safety for the creative and sometimes challenging longings of the soul to emerge. The movement from stage three to stages four and five is facilitated by shifting the central position of internal observation from the conscience to a nonjudgmental "witness."

This was certainly the case with Charlie. As he continued to set aside regular time for reflection, he began to experience more internal control over moving back and forth between stage-three processing of his external responsibilities and the more reflective witnessing of his internal world. His efforts to hold himself accountable and make amends to his wife and family for his role in creating problems for them eventually led to a decrease in the intense self-reproach that he had experienced earlier.

Reduced preoccupation with painful guilt allowed Charlie to pay attention to his marriage less from the point of view of a fault-finding critic and more through the eye of an inquisitive witness. Why had he chosen to spend so little time with Joyce? What had held him back from taking more time off work to attend some of the boys' school events? Why had he felt so embarrassed when, on graduating from college, he told Joyce that he would turn down the teaching job and work at the store?

When the witness is free to ask such questions with an attitude of nonjudgmental curiosity, it leads to the exploration of experiences, which in turn prompts responses that gradually take on the form and flow of stories. Elaboration of these stories can uncover helpful insights about ourselves that are embedded in the personal narratives. Thus Charlie entered into stages four and five of psychological reflection.

Stages Four and Five of Self-Awareness: The Development of Nonjudgmental Reflection

The essence of stage-four psychological reflection involves the practice of paying nonjudgmental attention to the actual stories of our life. The skills required to do this are first learned in the context of a relationship. We express our own personal experiences to another human being who is capable of listening with acceptance. Describing events in this caring environment first of all confirms that what happens to us during the day is important and worthy of consideration. In addition, if another person can listen uncritically, there is a good chance that we too might learn to listen to ourselves in that way. Though this process hopefully is first encountered and learned in childhood, there is no age limit that bars us from acquiring it at any point in our lives.

When we have the experience of people listening to what we are saying with an accepting attitude, it eventually frees the journalist in us to honestly describe what really happened. In the beginning, this emerging narrative might resemble a newspaper account in which reporters set out to weave the events of the day into a sequential form that sounds much like a story. Over time, however, this changes. Inevitably the storyteller in us parts company with anything that resembles a professional journalist.

Anyone who has repeatedly shared a personal story with other people has noticed how the facts may stay the same but the shape of the story gradually begins to change. Personal stories shared with others do not remain in the same set form. They receive slightly different emphases when told to various people in different contexts. Each story evolves over time, sometimes even taking on a different beginning, middle, or ending. This does not necessarily mean that the story is becoming any less true. Often it is quite the contrary. These kaleidoscopic fluctuations of personal narratives allow various patterns to emerge that may reveal new truths that were embedded in the relationships between seemingly unrelated occurrences.

People who tell a story often enough may even come to recognize and accept the evolution of its structure. They respect the dynamic and complicated life that lies at the heart of a story. They understand how shifts in progression or emphasis can be harbingers of different truths embodied in the same narrative. Personal stories, told repeatedly over a long time, inevitably become less of a mirror of objective reality and more a reflection of the storyteller's own subjective state. Therapists and spiritual directors have known for a long time that it is often not the person who is telling the story, but a presence within the story itself that is revealing something to that person about their life. When we learn to listen to stories in this way, we can begin to hear how there is often much more to a narrative than its surface intention to inform, impress, or entertain.

Over the course of his therapy, Charlie often found himself drawn back to a series of stories that clustered around a certain period of his life. The time frame was mainly bracketed within his early twenties. He was a junior in college, majoring in English, and just starting his practice teaching at a high school connected with the university. Learning how to organize and plan classes for a group of sophomores who had little interest in American literature was the biggest challenge he had ever faced. Despite the help of his mentor teacher, he sometimes failed, but the good days provided a rush of elation unmatched by anything he had felt before. Charlie laughed as he told me how he knew what Arthur Miller meant when he described a salesman as "a man way out there in the blue riding on nothing but a smile and a shoeshine." This is exactly what it is like to be a teacher, he said.

One day when he was telling me about similar experiences that had occurred around this time when he was in college, tears welled up unexpectedly in Charlie's eyes. I asked him what he felt. He was not sure. This reaction surprised him because it didn't fit. The college years had been challenging times, but they were often referred to as basically happy ones. As our time ended that day, we both agreed that these incongruous tears meant something important and that we would try to explore them as we continued in the sessions ahead.

The transition into stage five is heralded by the arrival of affect. As the events of the narrative are recalled, feelings and fantasies are drawn up to match with the words and phrases as though they were attracted to a magnet. The end result of this process is like musical notes becoming attached to words, transforming the story into song. When affect arrives, it animates the storyteller and the story changes again.

The feelings that rise to the surface in this way are usually predictable and even pleasant. They may lighten the tone of our story with humor, empower our anger, or cross boundaries of time and space to reunite us with loved ones in grief. Whether happy or sad, it is affect that gives resonance to our voice. When stories are shared with an authentic resonant voice, they can produce an additional effect of joining the heart of the storyteller to the heart of the hearer.

There are other feelings, however, that may come to our consciousness as a surprise or even a disruption. They also appear with their own timing and intensity, but they don't seem to fit with the story. They don't match up with our preconceived notions of what we thought the story was all about. Some of those feelings may be embarrassing or frightening. Others may even be overwhelming. We may find ourselves having a strong reaction to a seemingly minor incident and don't know why. We may be puzzled when angry feelings arise to meet a narrative that is bland or even humorous. It is very important to understand that when affect is incongruous with the story it does not mean that the affect is "wrong" or undeserving of attention. Avoiding seemingly inappropriate feelings only seems to provoke their relentless recurrence.

Charlie spent a good deal of time trying to make sense of the unexpected affect that emerged in connection with one of the happier periods of his life. He eventually interpreted the tears that welled up when he spoke about teaching as his "grief." He recognized the sorrow behind his decision to sacrifice his desire to be a teacher in order to please his father by going into training to take over the family business.

On the one hand, he was proud of the fact that, as the loyal oldest son, he had taken his dad's corner store and helped make it into what was now a bigger market and proud that his father could see this happen before he died. On the other hand, the decision to follow that path as well as to arrange his life around building the store had cost him his vocation as a teacher, his marriage, as well as his family life. Excessive hours at the store also had served to distract him from what was going on inside himself. The tears expanded as Charlie's heart opened and he poured out his grief.

In most cases, feelings are easy to include in a story because they fit with the intended theme. However, when the soul's affective input has been excluded for a long time its voice might no longer harmonize with even the main themes of the story. Charlie's soul had its own truth to tell and it would not rest until it was included. Its voice found allies when first Joyce then Susan confronted him with his overemphasis on work. When he stopped making excuses and reluctantly began to take to heart what they said, he saw the incongruity between the story he was telling about his happiness with his work and the presence of a nagging dissatisfaction he now recognized as grief.

People like Charlie, who are beginning to reflect on their life at stage four and stage five, will soon notice that there is no simple linear sequence to the progression of these stages. Sometimes the narrative part of the story appears first and then affect rises up to join it. At other times the opposite takes place, with affect emerging first and then some particular story later rising up into consciousness to match up with it. The process can begin with either stage four or stage five. When either stage is activated, it seems to rouse the other. The dynamic tension between these two stages invigorates the production of meaning and vitality in the psyche. One of the practical tasks associated with Charlie's progress in therapy involved his efforts to pair the stage-four events and stage-five feelings in both his past and current life.

The accurate joining of events and feelings is what the contemporary American psychologist Sylvan Tomkins called "affective associations." Each person's affective associations are like psychological fingerprints; no two people have exactly the same ones. Even when two people have shared the same objective experience, their subjective responses to it may be quite different. If this work of pairing events and feelings is left undone for a long period of time, people can experience such a discrepancy between what they are doing and feeling that they end up living in a house divided. The process of accurately fusing objective events and subjective responses provides the inner component of what we usually refer to as "integrity" (that is, "oneness"). To the extent that this integration is accomplished, the very distinction between "inner life" and "outer life" becomes a false dichotomy.

This is obviously not an easy task. The work of stages four and five demands making an effort not only to participate in one's life but also to reflect on it. Additionally, it requires an understanding that affect is one of the ways that the soul manifests itself in daily life. It progresses only when we begin to develop enough trust in our inner affective responses to include them as equal partners in creating the stories we tell about our life. Sometimes we may even be challenged by that affect to modify parts of a particular narrative so it matches more closely with what we truly feel. When a new story is formed, it may in turn prompt changes in how we decide to live our future life. What we are seeking to accomplish is that our external behavior eventually coincides more closely with the inner person we truly experience ourselves to be.

Stories become clearer as they are told in the company of others. In keeping with this, many men find it helpful to seek assistance at this point in the process. At about age thirty, Augustine was fortunate enough to meet two men who were very helpful to him as he set aside time to reflect on some personal questions and relate the stories that would eventually form a meaningful psychological and spiritual narrative for his life. Ambrose and Simplicianus stuck with him throughout this time and he was deeply appreciative of their presence. Charlie not only turned to me as his therapist, but also to his sister Gale, who lived in town and had been his closest sibling since they were children.

There is good reason to rely on selected friends, family members, support groups, or helping professionals for assistance and feedback whenever we take time to loaf and invite our soul. Few of us can go through this discernment process alone. It is so easy to avoid, distort, or deceive ourselves as we set out on any journey of personal discovery. These caring and accepting relationships are representatives of the larger community. Their very presence aids us in maintaining the focus, honesty, and compassion for ourselves that are sometimes difficult to sustain when we are faced with challenging new thoughts and feelings.

Three

Learning to Trust Our Soul as a Guide for Living

There is a delightful phrase in Italian that goes "...la dolce far niente—the sweetness of doing nothing." It expresses the sheer pleasure of loafing that Walt Whitman captured so sensuously in his poem "Song of Myself": "I lean and loaf at my ease observing a spear of summer grass." When the busy world is hushed, time stops and the senses sharpen. The conditions are right to invite the soul.

The soul accepts the invitation because it genuinely wants to be seen. Its basic nature is benign, and it seeks our attention primarily out of its need to be understood and be taken into account. One thing can be counted on: None of us has to go looking for the soul. If we sit still long enough, it will find us.

If invited, the soul emerges with the same freedom and abundance found in all of nature. It can be appreciated in the small pleasures and simple intrusions of everyday life. Becoming aware of its presence means paying attention to what is occurring in our peripheral vision. Feelings and fears, dreams and desires, fancies and fantasies are all vehicles for the soul's manifestation. At first, these momentary happenings may seem puzzling or even inappropriate, but that does not mean that they should be overlooked. The soul's appearances are not limited to what seems beautiful, timely, or easy to discern.

Problems can occur, however, if we do not loaf and invite our soul. If disregarded or neglected over a long period of time, its attempts at recognition can become troublesome. Charlie experienced his soul's relentless desire to be seen in the form of nagging feelings of dissatisfaction, problems sleeping, and persistent fatigue. These symptoms were the expression of a soul that had staked out residence in his daily life like an unwanted houseguest who refused to leave. It kept him up late and woke him up early. At the point of his divorce, it made even more noise. Charlie's soul did not demand to have its own way, but it did expect to be heard.

Augustine experienced his long-neglected soul's presence in the form of chronic restlessness. It took the joy right out of a very successful life. He also pointed out how the soul will actually attempt to "unmask us against our will." It does not follow rules and is unconcerned with fair play as it seizes upon any opportunity to reveal itself. Slips of the tongue occur with no respect for person or place. It also can make itself known by an ill-timed forgetfulness, an unplanned outburst, or a public stumble just as we reach for the award. The soul's agenda in such embarrassing incidents is not malicious. Its main desire is simply to be recognized and taken into account.

The soul has no respect for status. It will bother people who seem to have everything and it will also display little pity on those who have nothing at all. Rich or poor, celebrity or common folk, the soul shows no deference to what society might deem the "good life" or the "good person." It eventually finds its own way to unmask anyone proud enough to think that their success or goodness places them above listening to their own soul or that of another person.

One encouraging lesson that we might take from both Charlie and Augustine is that neither one of these men was born with some special skill for recognizing or understanding their soul. Like everyone else, they had to learn it. Unfortunately, both of them had already spent half a lifetime avoiding this process Their psychological awakenings eventually were prompted by personal tragedies, and not by some kind of attractive visions. What set them apart from many others, however, was that they reacted to these tragedies not solely as problems to be solved but also as rich experiences to be understood. Reflecting on their lives in this way led each of them to yet another level of self-observation that ultimately would involve acknowledgement of the soul itself.

Stages Six and Seven of Self-Awareness: Experiencing a "Psychological Conversion"

The repetitive work of associating affects and events, done in stages four and five, often leads to the unfolding of the next level of self-observation. Stages six and seven comprise a fundamental shift in the very manner that we approach our inner world. This transition can be summarized as a change of attitude by the witness from reflective observation of the soul to the formation of a trusting relationship with the soul. This move from analytical to relational processing might be called a "psychological conversion."

A psychological conversion involves two distinct steps. The first stage in this process is the recognition by the witness of a central core in the psyche that is usually called the "self" or the "soul." The second step involves the formation of a relationship between the witness and the soul in which the soul becomes a trustworthy resource for the guidance of one's life. Making such a psychological conversion does not supplant the self-understandings that still can be learned from the point of view of the previous stages. Rather, this transition may be seen as widening the scope of our vision so that we can appreciate all that our life has to offer from a fuller range of our awareness.

I don't want these last two stages to seem more uncommon
than they actually are. Anyone who has talked to himself in the
mirror knows something about paying attention to his soul. We
can understand the process that is involved here if we remember
those times when we looked ourselves in the eye and sincerely
asked a question: "Now what are you really feeling about X?"
There is an implicit recognition in this kind of eye-to-eye questioning and listening that somewhere within the mind is a self
beyond our social mask that has an honest response worth listening to. This experience has some basic elements in common
with the attitude taken by people who are open to sensing the
presence of their soul.

As we examine stages six and seven in more detail we will
look at how Charlie and Augustine each experienced this transition in their own unique way. We will also see how some men
find a sense of peace as a result of going through this process.

The recognition of a central core in the psyche is the prime
indicator of the sixth stage of psychological processing. It is an
insight that emerges from the persistent attention that we paid to
our inner world during the previous two stages.

The continued pairing of affect and events leads us to a gradual awakening that there is a remarkable likeness in our subjective responses to similar events. We eventually come to see that
our feelings are not as random and chaotic as they first appeared.
There are consistent threads and repetitive patterns that suggest
some creative organization in the process that produces them.
This formative process seems to operate somewhere beyond our
conscious awareness and control. It is as if there is a coherent
presence residing within each of us that continuously expresses
meaningful reactions to each life event through a unique and creative language composed of feelings, dreams, and fantasies.

People who experience this presence describe it as a kind of
vital core deep within themselves. Throughout history, individu-

als who were curious about their interior life have called this central point of activity by different names: "my soul," "my deepest center," "my true self," "the real me." Charlie described his experience of this inner process as his "soul." This key insight marked his transition to the sixth stage.

Charlie's preliminary recognition of the presence of his soul occurred in the course of his repeated exploration of a central question: How could he have let work so dominate his life that it caused him to lose his family? This challenging problem kept bringing him back to an earlier period of his life when, as a young adult, he made his first decisions about work. When he decided to accept the job at the store and forgo his desire to teach, he remembered the contrast between his father's elation at this decision and his own sense of feeling mainly relief. His future was now comfortably secure. He recalled again how he hadn't really talked this over with Joyce and later felt embarrassed when he told her what he had privately decided. As the years passed, his hard work at the store brought many successes but little satisfaction. He felt increasingly burdened, fatigued, and emotionally dulled. He didn't understand what this was about, but he did try to ignore the feelings and put up a positive front both to this family and himself.

Once he came into therapy and recognized this false image he was projecting, Charlie, in effect, began to look into the mirror and ask himself what he really felt. Going back to match his true feelings to specific events led him to a gradual awakening that he was finding similar subjective responses to the common theme of his work. His affective reactions were not as positive as he had previously portrayed, nor were they as confusing as they first appeared. In fact, they were becoming downright predictable. His fatigue, lack of emotional vitality, and sense of personal stagnation were all tied to the same theme: his job. In addition, he saw how all this overwork had served to distract him from acknowledging these persistent internal messages.

It became apparent to Charlie that these consistent and predictable responses were rising from a single source deep within himself. He eventually came to experience this source as a cohesive center that was not only creative but potentially helpful. In hindsight, he now saw that the nagging sense of unhappiness that he had felt for so long was actually his soul's attempts to be recognized and taken into account. He concluded that if only he had listened to the musings of this helpful inner resource much earlier, many of his past troubles and much of his present unhappiness might well have been reduced or even avoided.

Based on this insight, Charlie resolved to make a radical shift in his center of authority. He would reduce the high priority he had been placing on such external values as security and the opinions of others as guides for making decisions about his future life. His new desire was to include more of his whole self in this important process. This would mean increasing the trust that he would give to his soul's perceptions as he set out to reconstruct his future life.

Despite the mental efforts that this transition would entail, Charlie was gaining confidence that he had finally found a resource that could anchor his world and provide him with a means for understanding the past and planning his future. He described this inner work in terms of "coming home." He felt more energy flowing into his daily activities as well as a growing sense of peace that gave him a glimpse of hope.

The shifting of trust to the soul as an authority for guidance and meaning is the central feature of the seventh stage of psychological processing. Stage six had to do with the recognition of this central core self. At stage seven, there is not only an acknowledgement of the existence of that inner self, but also a placement of more trust in it as a guide for conducting one's life. People who have made this transition, and who speak about it in psychotherapy, sometimes begin to refer to their soul with additional descriptive terms such as "my inner compass" or "my guide." Some of these men have also described dreams in which their soul was personified as a wisdom figure such as a sage or healer or a wise old man who appeared and spoke to them.

Differentiating the voice of the soul within the complexity of the psyche is difficult enough. However, the process of distilling the multitude of its expressions into insights we can trust may prove to be an even more formidable task. This process of discernment is so hard to do and takes so much time because the reactions of the soul are complex and sometimes even blatantly contradictory.

In some ways, what we experience when we pay close attention to the voice of the soul is similar to what it is like when we pay close attention to scientific research. Reports of new discoveries that are recorded in professional journals are essentially printed versions of ongoing conversations that are being held between various scientists. What we overhear are the points, counterpoints, syntheses, and rebuttals that are being made by a group of people who are engaged in trying to unravel some particular scientific mystery. The term *most recent scientific finding* is not intended, even by its proponents, to be the final truth in the matter under discussion. It is merely a milestone that marks the latest progress of someone who knows he or she is treading a long and complex path.

When we ourselves write in a personal journal, what we are eventually recording are the internal conversations of our soul. What we are overhearing are the soul's most current impressions of whatever might be important at that time. Later, if we reread what we have written, these recorded messages will probably sound contradictory. Like the scientist, the soul does not *have* the truth, but engages itself in honestly *seeking* it. As new data are taken into account, the soul's opinions are refined or even changed, but eventually patterns do emerge that can be helpful in guiding our life. However, also like scientific research, there is never going to be a final "product." The soul will always be in process. Truth is always unfolding.

Augustine felt that we should trust the soul in the same way that we trust our senses. He considered the soul to be like a sixth sense that is closely related to those of the physical body. "So, step by step, my thoughts moved on from the consideration of material things to the soul, which perceives things through the senses of the body, and then to the soul's inner power, to which the bodily senses communicate external facts." He wanted to learn how to listen with the "ears of my soul," to look with the "eye of my soul," to smell, taste, and touch in this much more subjective way. His description of how he was transforming his awareness of the world around him is consistent with anyone who is trying to learn how to include the perceptions of their soul in the more general ways that they examine their life.

It is here, at stage seven, that the transformation taking place truly can be called a "psychological conversion." At this point, we set out on a course that goes beyond simply recognizing and listening to the soul's voice and start to trust it enough to begin altering our life based on its unfolding perceptions. Trusting this vital center as a guide requires an understanding that the soul is not the object but the subject of our life's passage.

Anyone who takes this step rounds a corner that offers a very different perspective. What is left behind is any reflexive use of external social expectations as the main compass for managing our daily life. The soul offers a more dynamic alternative. Trusting it means opening ourselves to more spontaneous, lively, or even playful ways of living our current life.

As this inner life of feelings, dreams, and fantasies becomes more relevant, creative alternatives for planning our future may also arise. Finding ways to honor those possibilities will allow us to feel less "stuck" or "trapped" in our present situation as well as open up new directions for our future. Even in the face of very dark circumstances, the soul can be counted on to offer some ray of hope.

At this point, there is yet another important reason for seeking the companionship of others when we loaf and invite our soul. Caring human contact activates the soul. Throughout our entire developmental history, our true self was most likely to emerge in the context of an accepting relationship. The companions that we choose to accompany us now replicate those original relationships that fostered our growth from the earliest years of our life. The emergence of the individual soul into the communal world has always depended on the invitations of the caring individuals who served as the attendants and sponsors in that transition. The same is true now, at whatever point we are in our development.

What Charlie experienced with his sister and with me in psychotherapy could be helpful because it replicated the kind of relationship that previously encouraged the emergence of his soul during earlier periods in his life. What Augustine experienced with Ambrose and Simplicianus likewise depended on the people who previously assisted in that process. The major difference, at this juncture in their lives, was that both men were no longer merely enduring their soul's relentless attempts to break down their masks and be seen. With the help of caring individuals, they were now recognizing its presence, learning how to listen to its voice, and actually beginning to place some trust in its perceptions.

Past relationships help us in understanding how this process works in the present. One way that we can recognize this vital creative center that seeks our attention today is by learning how to identify the various people who touched that center in our past. Once we can name these special people, we can more easily recognize the unique process that may promote the emergence of our soul today. A large measure of coming to better understand who we are is learning how to appreciate the enlivening of our psycho-spiritual life that happened in those previous caring relationships when we first came to be. That is our next step in examining this process.

Four

The Soul Begins to Emerge in Our Earliest Relationships

The soul does not emerge alone. It unfolds in the context of a series of distinctive relationships that optimally begin in the family but are potentially present throughout the entire life cycle. These relationships are so necessary for the soul's birth and growth that newborns arrive already predisposed to engage in them. The first signs of these vital connections can be seen in the physical dimension soon after birth.

The British psychoanalyst D. W. Winnicott frequently made the point that "there is no such thing as a baby." What he meant was that babies do not arrive in self-contained packages. The basic unit of life is not the baby but the baby-and-the-caregiver. An infant cannot be separated from the persons who physically and emotionally sustain it. This connection between the baby and the caregiver provides the basic context that is needed for its survival. The caregiver is as essential for the newborn's potential to thrive as the food he eats and the air he breathes. Furthermore, the infant arrives in the world with a built-in capacity to engage in this life-sustaining connection.

Babies are born hardwired to connect. They begin this connection within hours after birth by attaching to the world through their reflex to suck. Early survival takes place in the context of receiving nourishment through this relationship with another person. This life-giving physical connection also sets the stage for the subsequent psychological relationship.

Just as the mouth is the preliminary organ for physical connection, so the eyes become the preliminary organ for psychological connection. The prototype of psychological birth occurs when the infant's vision eventually drifts upward to focus on the face of the caregiver. This visual movement from breast or bottle to the face can be understood both literally and metaphorically as the first step in an important psychological process that will take decades to unfold.

The movement of the eyes to the face is the genesis of the eventual differentiation between "that-which-feeds" and "she/he-who-feeds." In other words, it is the first step toward our later ability to distinguish between the impersonal and the personal, the object and the subject. This distinction is what empowers us to treat another person, as the philosopher Martin Buber suggested, less like an impersonal "it" and more like a personal "thou." The movement of the eyes to the face is the initial progression in the long sweep of human development that culminates when we can eventually see other people less as objects for gratification and more as subjects for emotional affiliation.

The center of modern psychology might well be illustrated by the image of the human face. Winnicott referred to the faces of our parents as the first "mirrors" into which we looked to gain our initial sense of who we are. It was in the eyes of those who first accepted our upward gaze that we initially saw our own reflection and became conscious of what it meant to be fully alive.

These caregivers responded by returning the gaze. From the dawn of time, parents have focused on the eyes of their offspring and have coaxed, cajoled, teased, sung, laughed, and even wheedled them into the world. Human development requires not only biological but also psychological generation. Just as we were dependent on our parents for our physical birth, we were also dependent on their inviting gaze for the initial liberation of our psychological life. It was in their continuing gaze or its memory that our life has been sustained.

Augustine believed that this movement of the gaze to the face—from the impersonal to the personal—had implications for spiritual development. He illustrated the parallels between psychological and spiritual growth in the way that he structured the *Confessions*. The book is divided into segments based on the chronological progression of relationships with specific individuals who personally touched his heart. It begins with his mother, Monica, and follows through with his friends and finally his mentor, Ambrose. He showed how it was in the eyes of these attentive people that he began to understand the personal and subjective process that was also present in his own heart. Their deep care helped him develop a growing esteem for the personal center within himself that he eventually identified as his soul. He experienced his soul as not only enlivened by the presence of these other people, but reflexively reaching out to unite with the same core within each of them.

The focus on caring relationships as central to his psychological birth and development became a major theme for how he understood his spiritual maturation. Augustine believed, first of all, that at the center of the human heart is a restlessness for intimacy. He applied this psychological restlessness for intimacy to the spiritual dimension. From his point of view, the desire for what is deepest in me to unite with what is deepest in you is not only true of human relationships but is also the prototype for encountering the divine. He experienced this inborn hunger for true communion with another as the force that ultimately drew him to God, the very source of loving subjectivity. As he wrote in the *Confessions*, "Our hearts are restless until they rest in you."

Augustine wanted, above all else, to open his eyes and lift his gaze beyond the necessary but shortsighted world of simple physical comfort so that he could see the face of God. Just as the center for modern psychology might be illustrated by the human face, so the center of Augustine's spiritual world might well be illustrated by this very personal and loving image, which he experienced as the face of God.

Sponsors Play an Integral Role in the Process of Development

The image of coming alive in the gaze of another is the archetype of psychological and spiritual birth and growth. This experience hopefully began in the company of our initial caregivers. It is potentially present for the renewal and enhancement of each person's development throughout their entire life span. There is a name for those caring individuals who take the time to connect with the heart of another human being and ease that individual into the communal world. These important people might be called "sponsors" and the distinctive relationship that they provide may be seen as "sponsorship."

Churches have long recognized the importance of sponsors in the spiritual dimension. The sacrament of baptism, which celebrates the initiation of the individual soul into the Christian community, requires the presence of two people who are designated as the child's sponsors. These individuals stand with a hand extended in blessing over this new life that is being welcomed into the world beyond its family. They represent the intentions of the whole community to support that life.

It is important to distinguish between sponsors and parents because the child's ongoing psycho-spiritual development will also depend on people who are outside the bounds of the nuclear family. Even the most involved parents need the help of others in order to effect the psychological and spiritual maturation of their own children. This complex process certainly starts with good parenting, but it also requires a series of additional relationships with various people who will serve briefly, intermittently, or for extended periods of time in the special role of attending to the inner life of the child. The need for such individuals, both within and outside the family, is basic and primary to healthy psychospiritual development. It is as fundamental as the need for attachment itself. We are born dependent on the dynamic presence of sponsors to liberate the life that exists within us.

Sponsors do not give life, but affirm it. Their role is to bear witness to the life that is already present in each person at birth. By doing so, they assist in the emergence of another human being's subjective presence and, in effect, welcome him or her into the communal domain. This witnessing presence of the sponsor serves as the catalyst, the leaven, the transforming agent, the attendant at the threshold that is necessary to help bridge the gap between the inner world of private reverie and the outer world of communal engagement. This inner life that the sponsor affirms is referred to in modern times as the "self," but many people, like Charlie, still call it by the same term used during the time of Augustine: the "soul."

In the process of examining his life, it was quite natural for Charlie to begin identifying the specific people who had served as sponsors and censors during the course of his life. Unfortunately, he found a limited number of sponsors in his early history. In retrospect, he could see that the frequent conflicts with his mother that characterized his adolescence were far outweighed by her attentive presence that had sustained him during his early childhood. Though he remembers playing with his father, he was largely absent from Charlie's early memories, probably because of long hours spent at the store. He remembered few family friends who paid much attention to him. His preschool contact beyond the home was limited to relatives whose gatherings were apparently linked to holidays and a summer picnic. None of his aunts, uncles, or cousins stood out to him. There were memories of Sunday Mass and church activities, but he did not recall being touched by any of those group activities.

Charlie developed a new appreciation and gratitude for the role of his mother in nurturing some sense of an inner life for him during his earliest years. However, the arrival of his sister Gale, three years after he was born, would not only necessitate the sharing of Mother's attention but also date the time when he felt a painful fall from grace. Charlie never wavered from his perception that his mother much preferred having a daughter. Gale had not yet become the playmate, much less the confidante that would characterize their later relationship. With this early dearth of compatible people nearby and a mother distracted by a new baby, Charlie could better understand why he felt so lonely and gradually turned to mastery of external tasks for more dependable satisfactions.

Augustine's autobiography and Charlie's psychotherapy show several important similarities. Like many people who take the time to examine their own history, they both tended to structure their memories in segments based on connections with others. They each were able to distinguish some significant people who had played the roles of sponsors and censors in their lives. When the experiences with sponsors were placed in a rough chronological progression, this timeline offered a clearer perspective on the developmental process. The connecting thread was not tied to the external people but to an interior sense of agency that was struggling to come to life. What held all these experiences together was the presence of each man's soul, which was expressing consistently positive reactions to these people who were serving as its sponsors.

Charlie and Augustine were exploring their histories because they were trying to learn from their past mistakes. They shared a common error. Both previously had neglected their inner life to such an extent that they had undervalued these reactions to others. The reason for this inattentiveness was also strikingly similar. Each man was brought up in a home where there was limited appreciation of the inner life. They learned early on that rewards were primarily attached to mastery of external challenges such as school and work. Unfortunately, their neglected souls soon began to bother them in ways that would remain inexpressible until later in their adult years.

It wasn't until well into middle age that either man paid much attention to his interior life. As they explored their connections with others, they could better understand the communal nature of their individual souls. This private inner process could not be integrated into the interpersonal world by their individual efforts alone. There is no such thing as a self-made man. The emergence of their souls depended on the affirming acts of psychological hospitality provided by other people. In the early years of their lives, unfortunately, such opportunities had been limited.

Writing an autobiography or engaging in psychotherapy are excellent ways for any of us to trace the emerging path of our soul. Sometimes it helps to start from the outside and work in. We do this by examining our history for memories of particular people who were present for brief intervals or longer periods of time and now stand out in retrospect as the ones who touched our heart. These individuals, in whose eyes we came to life, provide us with a whole new kind of heritage. It is a background that actually could be illustrated in the form of a family tree. The soul has an ancestral lineage of its own. Its birth chart similarly is marked by "mothers" and "fathers" who assisted in the process of its emergence into the world. These special people comprise our own family tree of sponsors.

Augustine's *Confessions* provided him with a written record that he might well have set in a place of honor to remind himself of all those special people who assisted in the emergence of his life. Our own personal heritage of sponsors might also be found close at hand. They may be the ones in the photographs hanging on our walls or arranged above our desk. Sometimes the best place to start looking for sponsors is the family album. Somewhere there are pictures of those cherished individuals who were there when we needed them. Looking again at their faces, we remember their inviting gaze. Anytime we can identify the presence of these sponsors, we can more easily trace the progressive emergence of our soul.

Sponsorship Requires Safety: The Childhood Years

Sponsorship begins with safety. From a psychological perspective, the issue of safety is fundamental to any relationship. The first thing that any two people owe each other is safety. No level of intimacy can be sustained and no personal conflicts resolved in an environment where anyone feels unsafe. Sponsorship does not occur in the presence of threat because the soul will not emerge in an atmosphere of fear.

The experience of safety is not simply confined to freedom from physical abuse. Safety also requires the absence of all forms of verbal harm. Name-calling, hostile criticism, and raising one's voice to the point of intimidation are examples of behaviors that compromise safety. Likewise, nonverbal expressions of contempt, such as the silent treatment or emotional withdrawal, are essentially attempts at manipulation and control that have no place in respectful relationships. Our first responsibility as caregivers is the provision of safety for those in our care.

The relationship between the adults who live in the home provides the emotional container for the development of children. Some psychologists refer to this emotional container as the "holding environment" of the family. It is in this holding environment that the sponsorship of the next generation begins. The way and degree to which parents manage safety in their own relationship as well as between their children has a direct bearing on each child's freedom to grow.

Charlie grew up in a home environment where the functional aspects of his family life were adequately organized and responsive to his basic needs. The foundation for the emotional stability in the home was provided mainly by his mother. Though his father functioned at a high level outside the house and was a good provider, he was demanding and emotionally volatile at home. He was especially critical of Charlie's mother and responded with blame or punitive periods of silence if things did not go to his satisfaction. Charlie referred to this latter behavior as his "silent temper tantrums." He looked up to his father for his success at work, but felt fearful of him at home. Looking back, he recognized how he developed a consistent way of dealing with these fears from his earliest childhood years. He kept a low profile in the home and focused on his achievements at school in order to please him and avoid his wrath.

Charlie's father was more frequently hostile than he was angry. This is an important distinction. Anger is a normal feeling that will rise up from time to time in any close relationship. It benefits both parties when anger is put into words. If expressed in a healthy way, the angry feeling is clearly named and teamed up with the incident that caused it. This pairing of affect and event in the interpersonal expression of anger is similar to the same pairing of affect and event that was learned in stages four and five of our internal psychological processing. When it is expressed in this same noncritical way, we can more clearly communicate our own pain and how it is connected with specific behaviors of that other person.

Hostility is abusive and gives anger a bad name. Hostility is the expression of angry feelings in ways primarily intended to hurt another person rather than communicate one's own pain. In Rogers's terms, hostility could be seen as prereflective anger. At its most primitive level, the anger goes unexpressed because it is ignored, denied, or manifested in dark moods. At the next level, the angry feelings come out in ways that put the other person on the defensive, such as blame, hostile criticism, or threatening demands. When it reaches the point of using guilt, anger is expressed by punishment. The silent treatment or other manipulative attempts to intimidate by abandonment are examples of the punitive nature of hostile behaviors at this stage.

The behavior of Charlie's father is a good example of hostility. He used silence to punish his wife for her supposed shortcomings rather than express whatever he himself was feeling. His hostile criticisms and demands did more to make her feel bad than communicate whatever was hurting him. These behaviors, in turn, affected the safety of all his family.

Charlie not only felt unsafe but confused. He grew up without a clue as to how he could effectively communicate something so basic as his own anger. Everybody is "homeschooled." Each family is an educational institution where children are taught by example and instruction the basic course in Human Relationships 101. There are many important lessons to be learned, not the least of which is how to manage one's aggression. Charlie's "school" provided not only a poor learning model, but both his "teachers" had lost their moral authority to instruct on this subject because of their own inadequate management of aggression. They failed to adequately help him learn the complex process of expressing his private anger in ways that fit into a communal world. His solution was a secret vow not to be angry. He learned to stuff these feelings and comply because it was the best way he knew to feel safe. His parents had functioned more like censors than sponsors of this important process.

Augustine's problems with safety were more associated with his formal education. Entrance into elementary school marked the beginning of a long and difficult period in his life. Looking back, he drew the painful conclusion that his parents were so overidentified with his being successful that they neglected to provide him with the protection he needed to survive in a harsh educational environment. He dated his early schooling experiences as the point when he had to pay so much attention to his external safety that he abandoned his inner life.

One way for poorer people to get ahead in Roman society was through education. In Augustine's case, not only was the school curriculum planned largely with this ultimate purpose in view, but his family strongly subscribed to similar goals as well. His father, Patricius, clearly was invested in the upward mobility of his family and invested a good deal of money toward the higher education of his verbally gifted son. His mother, Monica, supported a good education, but spiritual development was also a high priority. In her customary role of peacemaker, however, she submitted to her husband's emphasis on Augustine's academic accomplishments and underrepresented her own values. Augustine perceived that "both of my parents were unduly eager for me to learn."

At this point in his development, Augustine did not fit into a high-powered academic environment. He expressed his dissatisfaction by exhibiting behavioral problems at school. He was not an active troublemaker; his early rebellious behaviors mainly took the form of passive noncompliance. He played games when he should have been working, and probably would be labeled in today's jargon as a smart kid who was also an "underachiever" and "not working up to his abilities."

The school system responded in ways that threatened his sense of security. They tried to correct these behavioral lapses through punishments. Augustine remembers, "I was constantly subjected to violent threats and cruel punishments to make me learn." Some of these punishments took the form of physical beatings. They did not, however, achieve their intended purpose. Instead they only served to engender fears that alienated him from authority. He referred to his childhood years as a time characterized by unnecessary "suffering and humiliation."

His parents, in turn, inadvertently contributed to his loss of safety. Their strong desires for his success appeared to blind Monica and Patricius from seeing his pain. They ridiculed his pleading for help at school. "My elders and even my parents, who certainly wished me no harm, would laugh at the beatings I got." He felt abandoned by the entire adult community. He cites this as the time when he first began to cut himself off from all this pain and fear by closing down inside. He lost a connection with his emotional center and felt directionless.

Both Charlie and Augustine felt that their safety had not been adequately protected during their childhood years. The consequences for each of their futures were enormous. Augustine dated the abandonment of his soul to his entrance into school because it was at that time he could no longer bear its pain. His subsequent focus on material success delayed his spiritual awareness. Charlie coped with the fear of his father by developing a self-protective style of "reading and pleasing:" reading his father's wishes, then pleasing him to avoid punishment. This external orientation led him to lose touch with his inner life, which later affected an important decision. After college, he bypassed his heartfelt desires to teach in order to please his father by accepting the job at the store.

Charlie and Augustine lived in their own versions of a threatening world that we all share. As children, we too depended on those in charge to create protective holding environments in our families, schools, churches, and civic organizations where we could grow up securely. As adults, the provision of safety is the first contribution that we make to foster the growth of those who are now in our care. As sponsors ourselves, it is our affirming gaze that ushers that soul into the community where it will find life.

Five

The Soul Is Enriched by an Expanding Community

The emergence of the soul continues to take place in the context of an ever-expanding circle of relationships. These relationships begin in the nuclear family, open out to religious and educational institutions, and continue on into the wider community. Each new personal encounter creates a potential occasion for an interested party to assist in the child's psycho-spiritual unfolding. Different personalities within the community draw out different parts of the child that easily might go unnoticed in even the best of parental environments.

Grandparents and godparents, favorite aunts and uncles, siblings, close family friends, and even babysitters are given the first opportunities for touching the inner life of the growing child. These people also will provide a continuity to the young person's expanding world by their presence at future developmental transitions such as birthdays, confirmations, school events, and graduations. In many families, these stages on the road to adulthood not only are acknowledged as they occur but also are honored over time in the stories and humor of the relatives and friends who attended the events.

It is in the child's best interests for the parents to foster these relationships. However, it is also important that they simultaneously extend their umbrella of vigilance in order to monitor the safety of each new connection. One way to build watchfulness into a routine is to establish a pattern of family meals where there can be regular discussion of what happened during the day. By initiating early on the expectation that the family not only eats together but also holds a conversation during the meal, parents set a precedent for sharing experiences in the inner circle. The information that emerges from these discussions allows the adults to extend their attention and supervision to the safety of their child's environment as it expands more and more beyond the home. Most importantly, the dinner table provides a place where children can expect to talk about their lives in an environment watched over by the affirming "gaze" of caring adults.

As a young person's world stretches past familial boundaries, the opportunities for sponsoring relationships are usually identified with people who take on designated role relationships in the child's education. The first adults who are most likely to serve in this capacity are teachers. Ask anyone to identify a favorite teacher and they probably will not simply pick the smartest one. More likely, they will choose a teacher whom they admired and who went out of his or her way to make a personal connection with them. They will describe how they became excited about learning something new on account of that person's interest in them. They may not report becoming the greatest achiever because of this experience, but did feel more of a lively curiosity that drew them a step further into the sheer joy of true learning. No matter how briefly, they came alive. This whole process is connected to the root of what education is all about. The very word comes from the Latin *e-ducare*, which means "to lead out." Favorite teachers do what any sponsor does; they draw us out of ourselves. In so doing, they foster a personal connection between our inner life and some part of the wider world around us.

Charlie was very fortunate to have a fourth-grade nun who took a special interest in him during what proved to be a critical time in his education. The first couple of times, it was embarrassing to be asked to stay after school and review the day's lessons. He soon realized, however, that Sister Bernard was interested in something more than spelling words correctly and improving poor reading skills. After one of their daily teaching sessions, she said she wanted to give him a gift because "she could sense his desire to learn." She showed him a book about a boy who played first base, just as he did, and who dreamed of growing up to play that position for the Boston Red Sox. It was his to keep. Charlie teared up as he told me that story. Sister Bernard had looked past all his mischievous behavior and, with this simple gift, showed him that she saw the boy who wanted to learn. As an adult, he dates his initial interest in literature to this experience. It led him to pursue English as a major in college. He told me that he will never forget Sister Bernard; he still remembers her by name in his daily prayers.

The same opportunities to bring forth the inner life of a child are available to members of other helping professions. Clergy, school nurses, social workers, guidance counselors, police officers, physicians, and therapists also are professionals who are each trained to do a specific job and can be conscious of the possibility that they might serve in the wider role of sponsor for some of those who seek their care. Many coaches and scout leaders likewise understand their potential to touch the vitality that lies within the young people under their tutelage. Some of the men and women who take on these roles believe that winning a game or learning a skill is important, but not as primary as the life lessons that are being learned by the athletes on their team or the scouts in their troop. This attitude goes a long way toward noticing and opening up possibilities that something more can happen. Sponsors stand for the importance of a dimension in life that is just as worthy of attention as the promotion of achievement and success.

Sponsors do more than instruct, coach, mentor, or guide. They mediate development through their appreciative interest in the inner life of the person who stands before them. When we look back on our own lives, we can identify our sponsors not as the people who told us who we ought to be, but the ones who took the time to see and hear who we really were and are. They touched something in us and we came alive in their presence. We felt their appreciation and we began to understand that what may have seemed so unacceptable or unique in us might actually be welcome and have a place to fit into the larger community. Sometimes this can happen without any conscious intent on the part of the sponsor. Even designated sponsors, such as clergy, teachers, and therapists, often are surprised by what someone later told them was helpful about their involvement.

Designated or not, sponsors are found wherever communities are formed. They exist in the so-called good neighborhoods and bad. They may be of any race, religion, gender, age, socioeconomic status, or physical ability. They usually are not spotted by charisma or acclaim. Some appear only for a brief critical moment, while others may be available for extended periods of time.

The presence of sponsors is universal because the need to witness and be witnessed is universal. The longing to make one's grasp of things true before the eyes of another lies not only at the very beginning of human development but is intrinsic to psychospiritual growth throughout the entire life span.

Witnesses are needed most of all by anyone going through a developmental transition in his or her life. School passages, leaving home, moving, job entry, marriage, divorce, childbirth, and retirement are examples of markers for times when people are most vulnerable. Many are making decisions that will affect the rest of their lives. Whether that person is a child, adolescent, young adult, middle-aged person, or older adult, no one outgrows the need to have someone be with them to affirm the inner importance of their external transition. From a psychological point of view, we are more likely to turn to our own soul for guidance when we are standing in the attentive presence of a witness.

Sponsors Are Essential to Identity Formation during Adolescent Years

Much of a child's early life is occupied with this process of gaining proficiencies in the uncountable number of basic skills that he will need later when he functions as an adult. In his book *Childhood and Society,* Erik Erikson points out that after the advent of puberty and some initial mastery of these tools and tasks, childhood proper comes to an end. It is at this point that youth begins.

Erikson believed that the major challenge of this next developmental period is that of making an initial clarification of one's sense of identity. He did not offer any precise definitions of what he meant by that term. Rather, he described how the process itself is most commonly evidenced in a particular set of questions that many of us remember having first considered seriously when we were part of that age group. "Who am I?" "What do I want to do with my life?" These questions are concerned with the "vision" phase of identity formation.

Identity formation is not a static but a dynamic process that is characterized by a sense of the future. One word that captures this essential element of the future in identity is *vision.* The identity vision is a creative and imaginative contemplation of who we want to be. It is not simply "Who am I?" but "Who am I to be?" In this way, the word *identity* is not a noun but a verb, and one that is cast in the future tense. At this stage, it is not rational, logical, or even practical. It is often no more clear than simply an intuitive hunch.

Erikson wrote about how this process of identity formation is not confined to an internal monologue, but takes place in the framework of a much more complex social dialogue. A common theme that runs through his work in this area is the importance of the "face" in the ongoing development of human identity.

Adolescents crave the presence of adults who take an interest in their lives. Erikson pointed out that when these concerned individuals are absent, it is often the teenager who is first to notice and criticize the "facelessness" of modern society. Conversely, when adults take the time to truly engage one-on-one with adolescents, they are frequently amazed by the appreciation that is expressed for this "face-to-face" contact.

Erikson's focus on the face reminds us once again of the lifelong importance of the "gaze" in the process of our true self coming alive. The emergence, clarification, and sustaining of our identity takes place through a series of interpersonal dialogues. Adults who interact with youth and understand their role beyond skill enhancement can enter into these ongoing dialogues and participate as true sponsors of the psychological and spiritual development of the young people in their care.

The church has been long aware of the importance of identity formation in adolescence and its communal context. The sacrament of confirmation is usually conferred at the onset of the adolescent years, thus marking the transition into this important new developmental era. Among the key features of this timely sacrament is the opportunity for the recipient to choose a new name. This choice of a name signifies the challenge to actively discern one's true identity. The name traditionally is chosen from the roster of saints. Having the name of a saint is a reminder that the vision of who we are can include the ideals of who we aspire to be. It also provides a connection to a lineage of all those who have preceded us in taking up the inner work of discerning the voice of their soul. Once again, a sponsor is chosen to represent the wider community as it accompanies the recipient on this next step of his psycho-spiritual journey.

In keeping with what we know about identity formation, the role of this sponsor becomes increasingly effective if the accent of the dialogue is placed less on what the sponsor can put in and more on what he or she can draw out. When religious development is confined primarily to teaching a creed, then faith becomes synonymous with belief. A true sponsor is a witness, one who has more self-revealing questions to ask than set answers to provide. "What are you learning about your own spiritual path?" "How do your connections with others fit into your spiritual life?"

Questions posed in this manner prompt the young person to enter his faith community in a very different way. They help him to see the common ground he shares with adults further along on a spiritual quest of their own. He learns a fundamental feature of psycho-spiritual development: that when he becomes a true witness to the rich inner life in his own soul, he joins even more deeply with other members of his community. Together, they might be of some help to each other as they try to open their eyes and lift their collective gaze to a dimension of life that transcends even themselves and enters the realm of the spirit.

Augustine suffered from an insufficiency of witnesses at this point in his life. His adolescence was functionally successful but, to a large extent, psychologically and spiritually stagnant. His father was a good provider, but he was an inadequate witness to the inner life of his son. His parents' relationship was marred by his father's affairs and his verbal abuse. Augustine maintained close friendships with his peers, but spoke of no connection to his siblings or extended family. He mainly felt afraid of and alienated from his teachers. Any nourishing and sustaining emotional attention from an adult appears to have come solely from his mother. Without her, he might have despaired. Although he eventually credited Monica with being one of the primary sponsors of his spiritual life, as an adolescent she represented a church that was externally remote to her son and she wasn't able to teach him how to appreciate the inner gem.

Charlie was becoming more aware of the psychological and physical changes that were happening to him as an adolescent.

He tried to understand what was going on with his body, but he often felt out of control and he found no one to turn to for guidance. He felt embarrassed and confused by his sexual feelings. The explanations that he was receiving from school were insufficient and everyone else seemed to be understanding this whole thing much better than he was. He felt alone.

Charlie's parents provided him with little helpful guidance or understanding. In fact, he recalled an experience with them that remained a prominent memory into adulthood and one that he felt characterized their attitude toward his sexuality. When he was about sixteen years old, his father noticed that Charlie was having an erection. His response was to laughingly comment about how much he looked forward to having some grandchildren. Later, he told Charlie's mother about the incident in his presence. She reacted with alarm and apprehension. Charlie felt mortified and could hardly face either of them for weeks.

Charlie's father was a witness to the biological awakening of his son's sexuality and his laughing report of it brought up anxiety in his mother. Unfortunately, these responses are examples of how discussions of adolescent sex become overly focused on the external physical changes and too often ignore the feelings and needs of the boy himself. Mother's response of alarm illustrates a common reaction of authorities to emerging male sexuality: worry and fear. Father's self-referencing comment and Mother's anxiety distracted them both from asking Charlie how he felt about the important changes happening in his body. No one acted to ease his private juvenile concerns into the public realm of mature adults where he could have received guidance. An opportunity was lost.

This was not a unique or isolated experience. Charlie alluded to other less dramatic examples that confirmed such responses were typical of his parents' reactions to his sexuality. The repetition of these themes very likely contributed to the formation of

Charlie's personal attitudes toward sex. He learned to process his emerging sexual life through the anxious eyes of his own internal critic. This set the tone for decades of fear, confusion, guilt, and shame about being a sexual person. He learned early on to hide these feelings rather than discuss them.

The very adults who served as sponsors and mentors for Charlie's social and intellectual life also inadvertently served as censors for his sexual life. Censorship, like sponsorship, starts on the outside. Some people, often more out of ignorance than maliciousness, can respond repeatedly in ways that confuse, retard, or even inhibit important transitions in a young person's development. Fearful parents, guilt-inducing clergy, and overly restrictive educational systems can function, in effect, as censors that impede psychological growth. If censors arrive in a child's life during critical learning periods, they can have long-lasting effects because their voices become internalized and live on in the mind as a confusing and repressive force that counters the vital life of the soul.

Clarifying his sense of self as a sexual person is only one part of a much broader spectrum of issues encountered by the adolescent during this time of identity formation. When we, as adults are faced with the challenge of fostering the emergence of the inner life of the young people in our care, it helps to know what issues they are facing in each developmental stage. The psychologist Alfred Adler pointed out three major areas key to the construction of a sense of personal identity: work, intimate relationships (including sexuality), and group affiliation. The adolescent's unfolding notions of who he is to be in these three areas carries implications for present and future psycho-spiritual development.

Each seemingly practical choice made during the teen years is tied to larger psychological and spiritual questions. At the heart of an adolescent's identity formation is the discernment of his soul's preferences. When he is exploring job alternatives, the face value of his questions involves practical concerns about finding a livelihood. From the point of view of his psychological and spiritual life, he is dealing with his soul's musings about the choice of a vocation: What does he feel "called" to contribute?

His questions about attraction to another person are certainly about sexuality, but they also involve defining preferences for compatibility and learning how to channel true emotional intimacy into relationships. These concerns are connected to the larger dimension of his soul's longings for closeness in friendships, a possible commitment in marriage, and ultimately the quality of his relationship with God.

Questions about extracurricular activities at school may focus on a decision between joining the debate or basketball team. The choice of one over the other helps define and refine his soul's preferences for social-identity groups. Thoughtfully considering where he might truly fit in carries helpful implications for later in life when he will be faced with similar options as he seeks compatible communities to support his ongoing psychological and spiritual needs.

Adolescents benefit from talking about these quandaries with caring adults who have been through this before and recognize the larger implications of seemingly small decisions. There are many practical ways that we can function as sponsors, encouraging adolescents to include the creative voice of their soul as they clarify what they want while stumbling through this labyrinth of decisions. Most of all, young people do not benefit from judgments, analyses, or unsolicited advice that promote premature foreclosure of this vital process. In our own development, many of us did not find it helpful when people said our dreams about a job were "unrealistic," our best friend was "inferior," or that we had to stick it out to the end in every group in which we signed up to participate.

Parents cooperate during this developmental period by encouraging their adolescent to try out different alternatives, knowing that there is only limited time remaining for those daily kitchen table discussions where they can support and monitor the ongoing process. If a particular relationship is not a threat to our child's safety and he insists on pursuing it, we may be of better assistance by letting him learn from a potential mistake. We can help him explore what he wants rather than criticize it. Within parameters of common sense, it is better to allow young people to try out and quit groups and relationships. Valuable learning can take place if they are encouraged to understand, discouraged from acting impulsively, and helped to explore and accept the consequences. It will be easier for children and adolescents to learn loyalty when they have a better sense of where they choose to be loyal.

The adolescent also clarifies his vision of who he is by vicarious identification with heroes and villains. The choice of whose pictures he puts on his wall provides a series of mental rehearsals designed to test out how any given attractive self-definition might play out if it were enacted over time. Conversely, his adversaries sharpen the sense of who he is by comparison-contrast with who he isn't. Sports and entertainment figures as well as perfectly well-meaning people, even like ourselves, are sometimes chosen to play either role. These choices may change like the weather; today's hero may become tomorrow's villain. If we adults understand the psychological process that is going on behind those idealizations and devaluations, we might see their value and not take them so personally. In that way, we can be better equipped to listen and explore what all this means with less criticism and defensiveness.

Although identity formation is a primary and conscious pre-occupation of adolescents, the process did not begin nor does it end within this age group. As infants, our first "work" choices and experiences took place with toys, our first "intimate relationship" was with our primary caregiver, and our first "group affiliation" took place in connection with our family. As young children, we expanded our world of work and groups outside the home as we entered school. Ask almost any elementary school child what he wants to be when he grows up and he will answer in a way that shows he has given some prior thought to that question. Ask him to name his best friend and he will know exactly what you mean and have a response to your question about intimacy. At midlife, we have a lot in common with our adolescents as we make a more mature reexamination of our own work, intimacy, and place in the community. The standards against which these choices are now judged are not only our current success and happiness, but also how well they conform to the life we envisioned when we ourselves were adolescents. As we retire and grow older, we will be no less concerned about doing something that is worthwhile, feeling a special love for and from another person, and being part of a family, church, or any group that accepts and respects our presence.

Charlie and Augustine "graduated" from their basic "homeschooling" to enter the wider world with different levels of readiness. Augustine left his village for a big-city school in Carthage in order to study law, primarily because that was what bright boys did. There was no sense of vocation to his job preference. Though he had close male friends, the role of a community was to provide connections for success. Externally, he looked for all the world like a lucky young man. Inwardly, he felt lost and restless. Although Charlie was not the academic equal of Augustine, he went on to a Michigan college with a distinct sense of vocation. Attracted to teaching and interested in English literature, he felt a sense of purpose that covered his guilt and loneliness. Both men, however, were about to make major mistakes in their early twenties, mistakes that could have been avoided had they learned to be more in touch with their souls.

Six

The Soul Continues to Unfold during Our Adult Years

We want to unfold. That's how Rilke put it in his poem entitled "Seven." "I want to unfold. I don't want to stay folded anywhere, because where I am folded, there I am a lie. And I want my grasp of things true before you." These words capture the model for a lifetime of development; our soul yearns to emerge and be seen. It is a poem especially fitting for anyone in his twenties. The central developmental task for the young adult is to unfold the true longings of his soul into relationships and work.

Just as the psycho-spiritual work of adolescence was to clarify a sense of personal identity, the challenge of the twenties is to unfold that identity into a new and unique life. The choices and decisions made by the young adult work best in the long run if they conform to the visions of identity gained during his adolescence. Just as adolescence was a time of discernment, young adulthood is a time of commitment.

Statistically, it is during the decade of the twenties that most people will commit themselves to a primary relationship and make choices about the line of work that they will pursue as adults. The challenge during this period is to make those commitments with binocular vision. One eye must be focused closely on the array of practical choices in the external world. The other eye must remain attentive to the soul, which provides the vision for who we are to become.

The key to success in the twenties is to keep one's feet moving. The course we follow has a lot in common with an earlier time in our lives when we learned to walk. The educational paradigm is the same: trial and error. The process inevitably involves stumbling, progress is rarely linear, it takes time, and it usually makes parents and sponsors nervous if they watch. The decade of the twenties is often a time when the old maxim can prove alarmingly true: There is no road and one makes one's own road by walking.

Negotiating the young-adult period of development requires patience on both sides. The young person must learn to tolerate the ambiguities of his vision and try to make compromises that tread the fine line between being faithful and yet flexible in carrying out the vision. He must face fear and master the courage to try. He must notice success, admit failures, and know when to revise his strategy if the current plan isn't working.

It is best for parents and other sponsors to restrain themselves from excessive helpfulness. In particular, they must recognize that aid need not automatically take the form of material or functional assistance. It is just as important to provide encouragement and a listening ear when the young person becomes discouraged or needs to sort out his options. Sometimes it is better not to interfere reflexively by giving advice or resources unless asked or if the situation becomes unsafe. Many longer term problems are caused during this developmental period by well-meaning adults who are determined to be "helpful" because they themselves are invested in their offspring avoiding mistakes or proceeding along an orderly path. In trial and error learning, if we deprive someone of making errors, we inhibit his progress in learning. We adults must be very careful not to pressure our loved ones to pick a relationship or career because of our own needs. Likewise, we assist in keeping our postadolescent's feet moving by not bankrolling protracted vacillation.

Problems come to pass for the young person if he can no longer tolerate making errors and becomes so anxious that he stops taking reasonable risks. Erikson said that this usually happens in one of two ways: by diffusion or foreclosure. Identity diffusion occurs when the person handles his distress by prolonged indecision about longer term goals. In other words, these individuals stop moving their feet and the whole process stalls. Identity foreclosure happens when the young person manages his distress simply by coming up with a practical "solution." For example, he picks a reasonable or convenient person to marry or a work direction to follow because it is time to do so. If handy choices turn out to be sufficiently compatible with his soul's vision, then he may be on his own path by sheer luck. If his choices turn out to be primarily expedient, as was the case with both Charlie and Augustine, then the stage may be set for subsequent problems.

Each of these men resolved the developmental challenges of his twenties by employing the same ill-fated process: identity foreclosure. Charlie made decisions at age twenty-two that simply excluded following any avenue connected with his adolescent vision of becoming a high school English teacher. Augustine was forced by financial necessity to make some practical career choices that cut him off from looking at a larger array of options that would have been open to him.

The decision to work in retail foods allowed Charlie to take the next step on a familiar path that dated back to his after-school and summer jobs since age sixteen. He was lucky to have met Joyce during his junior year in college, and they both knew they wanted to get married right after graduation. As an accountant, her skills were portable and she was willing to move back to his hometown. After the two boys were born during their parents' late twenties, Charlie began more regular attendance at the same Catholic church where he had grown up. He saw later how his work choice had provided him with a convenient and secure platform for launching his adult life, but it completely neglected his soul's vision of teaching, thus setting him on a course marred by dissatisfaction for years to come.

Augustine's father died when he was about eighteen years old. This precipitated a financial crisis that had implications for his choices related to employment during the next phase of development. He felt pressure to foreclose on considering various work possibilities. Instead, he opted to take the qualifying exams to become a teacher. This allowed him to get a job and thus relieve his mother of the financial burden of supporting him.

At about age twenty, Augustine left Carthage and went back to his home town of Thagaste to begin his career teaching grammar and rhetoric. He brought along a woman with whom he had fathered a son named Adeodatus. Almost immediately he fell into conflict with his mother. The devout Catholic Monica was deeply upset that her son had left the faith. Their differences escalated to the point where she would not even sit at the same table with him. After a year he and his companion left Thagaste and moved back to Carthage, where he settled down for the rest of his twenties. He worked as a teacher and helped raise their son, while suffering what he later described as a constant sense of "restlessness."

Both Charlie and Augustine had now made the decisions about work and a primary relationship that are considered the external markers for completion of the psychological tasks associated with early adulthood. Charlie married Joyce and took the job of assisting his father in management of the family store. Augustine began his career in teaching. Although he was not in a formally committed marriage, he did pledge himself to sexual monogamy and participated in raising their son.

Each man was now entering his own version of the adult period of development. This is a time when day-to-day life usually takes on some routine and is experienced by many men as more stable and predictable than the transitional twenties. The psycho-spiritual comfort level of the thirties depends on the extent to which the choices made in love and work conform to the visions of identity garnered during adolescence.

The Challenge of the Adult Years Is to "Maintain the World"

Commitments to work and love relationships as well as participation in the social and faith communities that support those choices are the external markers of adulthood. These decisions lead the fledging adult into an enlarged circle of obligations with new social accountabilities. The ensuing challenges are different from the previous ones because this expansion of responsibilities requires an entirely different mind-set.

The determining factors in the transition to adulthood are not limited to the exterior and chronological, but also include subjective features. External changes in love and work prompt a shift in the internal world. The person going through this process senses that he is not just taking on some new set of duties, but also entering a new social role. It amounts to an understanding, which usually occurs sometime during the early phase of the adult years, that he is now joining the "generation in charge." It is this subjective recognition that marks his developmental passage. It requires taking on a different attitude as he accepts his new identity as an adult.

Erikson described this transition into adulthood as the move from functioning mainly in a "learning" position in society to one where there is a greater sharing of "teaching and instituting as well." He used a rather dramatic phrase to describe the challenges faced by anyone who takes this next developmental step. He referred to it as entering the generation of those who are now responsible for "maintenance of the world."

Erikson did not mean by this lofty phrase that one must do something great or rise to some distinguished position. Social status is not the issue here. It does not matter whether one's new sense of accountability involves doing tasks deemed by society as important or menial. Erikson mainly was trying to point out the fact that much of the heavy lifting in any community is done by its members who have reached the age range roughly spanning the thirties to the sixties. Prior to this time most people are primarily learning the ropes. Sometime after the age of sixty, many of us are beginning the process of handing over those ropes to the next generation.

It is this gradual inner acceptance that one is now in charge of something and thus responsible for maintenance of the world of one's choice that marks the transition into the developmental period of adulthood. The decade of the thirties is usually a time when prior growth is consolidated. The decisions that were made in the twenties are being refined on a day-to-day basis. Adjustments to work and accommodations to maintaining a marital and family life are the focus of attention for the young adult. To a large extent, satisfaction in the thirties depends on two factors. The first is the degree to which his external choices in love and work feel compatible with the inner person he senses himself to be. The second involves his willingness to put in the time and effort for both his work and intimacy to thrive. Sustained attention to these two areas will lay the foundation for his future years of adult life.

Even though Augustine and Charlie were both successful adults, each felt quite discontent in his thirties. Unfortunately, neither took the time to examine the inner roots of his dissatisfaction. They both simply tried to solve their difficulties by converting them into external problems and then making ill-considered adjustments to their day-to-day life.

Despite his success, Charlie felt a nagging sense of unhappiness. He sometimes wondered if his work was on the right track, but didn't want to face the possibility that he had made a mistake in choosing to return to the family business. Consequently, he resolved his internal dissatisfaction by converting it into an external problem. He then went on to solve this problem by renewing his commitment to the store and throwing himself even more vigorously into that work. This, unfortunately, confounded his difficulties. It took even more time away from Joyce and the boys, which gradually contributed to the deterioration of his marriage.

Augustine was becoming increasingly disenchanted with the whole process of teaching. However, instead of seeing this reaction as reflecting anything going on in himself, he blamed it entirely on his students. His complaint was that they were a rowdy bunch of unmotivated troublemakers. This may well have been true, but focusing on this solely as an external problem distracted him from also looking at what was going on in his own heart. He would solve this problem by getting another job. Leaving his family behind, he departed for Rome to seek housing and better work. Italian students would certainly be of better quality than North Africans.

Immediately after arriving in Rome, things went badly. Augustine experienced a tragedy that stopped him in his tracks in more ways than one. He became so seriously ill that he almost died. Deprived of his family, his large group of friends, and the distractions of his work, the normally gregarious Augustine ended up spending most of his time alone. During those idle hours, he found himself unwillingly dragged inward where he came face to face with memories of his conflicted past.

He did not like what he saw. This first encounter with his inner world was dominated by guilt. To begin with, he had treated his loving mother badly. He had lied to her, was ungrateful for her sacrifices, and responded to her sincere religious beliefs with condescension. He recalled his own history of rowdiness at school and disrespect even for helpful authorities. He had stolen from his neighbors and participated in a gang that acted violently. What's more, he had rationalized so much of this behavior, seeing himself as excepted from the rules because he was special and smarter than other people. He later identified this attitude as his "pride."

The lengthy illness, combined with the threat of death hanging over his head, prolonged and intensified Augustine's inward journey. Later on, writing in the *Confessions*, he identified this as the first instance when he had ever shifted his attention from the outer world of tasks and intellectual studies to the interior life of his psyche. It was a time of intense physical and psychological pain, borne in loneliness and touching on despair.

From the point of view of modern psychology, we can see how Augustine was making a major shift in his psychological processing. Previously accustomed to looking at his experience through the lens of Rogers's second stage (life happens on the outside of the psyche and can be solved like an exterior problem), he had now come face-to-face with his inner world. Like Charlie, his first encounter with his interior life was dominated by the presence of guilty recriminations. Augustine had now shifted to stage three of psychological processing and the "critic" was out in full force. Everything was simply good or bad, right or wrong. Alone and lacking the wider viewpoint of a compassionate "witness" in his life, the mental anguish must have seemed like an unending nightmare.

As time passed, Augustine recovered his health and began a new job of teaching grammar and rhetoric in Rome. The psychological experience he had endured during his illness remained in his memory but faded into the background. His mind turned once again to the demanding work of lesson planning and class-room teaching. He soon discovered that the grass was not greener in Rome. Students there brought discipline problems of their own. He was growing discouraged about finding a teaching job where he could concentrate on class work and pay less attention simply to maintaining order. He grew restless and even started to question his choice of career. However, he wasn't yet ready to pursue those feelings and doubts in order to trace their origins within himself.

After only a year in Rome, Augustine heard of a job opening in Milan for a teacher of literature and elocution and immediately applied. He was accepted and quickly arranged to move on once again. We don't know whether he was aware that this outer move might also be mirroring an inner transition. However, as he made that trip to Milan, he must have at least suspected that his rest-lessness could not be solved simply by making geographical changes. These feelings of discontent had traveled with him from Carthage to Rome and they would certainly follow along as he embarked on this next step of the journey. We do know that he now made his way with a new consciousness of the power resid-ing within his inner life. In Milan he will finally discover the sponsor he needs to help that inner life unfold.

Seven

Spiritual Awakening and Conversion in the Life of the Soul

Augustine arrived in Milan at age thirty. After two consecutive job disappointments, this was his third city and third place of work in as many years. In addition, the connection with his mother was apparently still strained. Questioning his career and the relationship with the woman with whom he had been living, Augustine lacked a vision for his future life in both work and love. He was deeply distressed.

He did benefit from the presence of a small community. It took the form of two old friends, who shared the common bond of dissatisfaction with their current lives and the search for a more meaningful future. These men joined Augustine in Milan "for no other purpose than to live with me, so that we might be together in our fervent search for truth and wisdom." It was truly a case of misery reaching out for company and seeking answers for shared problems. "We were like three hungry mouths, able only to gasp out our needs to one another."

Augustine supported himself through his new job of teaching public-speaking skills to lawyers. However, the confident and proud demeanor that had characterized his attitude in North Africa was gone. Since Rome, his attention was focused more on his troubled inner life than outer achievement. He described himself as "bewildered," "floundering" and tempted to "despair." All this emotional pain prompted him to do something that he had never done before—to seek help for his personal problems.

Soon after his arrival, Augustine went to the local cathedral to hear a man named Ambrose speak. Ambrose was the bishop of Milan, a respected leader in the community, and well known for his skills as a talented orator. Although Augustine had gone to a church to hear someone talking about religious matters, he told his friends that he was attending these services for professional reasons. He said he was researching a different oratorical style and had no interest at all in religion. After listening to the sermon, Augustine reviewed the speaker as a learned man with a "charming delivery, though not soothing and gratifying." Despite this tepid evaluation, he was sufficiently impressed to return.

Ambrose customarily made himself available after Mass in a corner of the cathedral so that people could easily approach him with their problems. As time went on, Augustine found himself also wanting to have one of those private conversations. He began to search for an opportunity "to pour out my sea of troubles before him." However, there were usually so many other people lined up waiting to present their own problems that he had to wait his turn and settle for brief encounters.

After a series of short private conversations, Augustine felt even more favorably impressed. His initial assessment of Ambrose was that he was a person of genuine kindness. "My heart warmed to him, not at first as a teacher of truth, which I quite despaired of finding in your church, but simply as a man who showed me kindness." As Augustine spent additional time with him, he was clearly becoming more personally attached. He even began to describe Ambrose in terms that reflected a growing sense of mutual closeness: "This man of God received me as a father." Augustine had finally found a "teacher of truth," who treated him with kindness and understood him in ways that brought his despairing soul to life.

Ambrose Becomes a Sponsor for Augustine: The Bridge between His Intellect and His Heart

The external limitations of the relationship between Ambrose and Augustine stand out in a striking contrast to the powerful generative effect it began to have on Augustine's psycho-spiritual life. In the first place, this was not primarily a personal relationship, but one that was structured within a professional role. Secondly, even though they continued to meet over a period of about three years, there would be relatively few private moments spent together. Despite these limitations, this relationship was becoming the catalyst that enlivened a powerful process deep within Augustine's psyche.

As he continued to pour out his troubled thoughts and feelings, a core theme emerged in the counsel he received. The message itself was deceptively simple. Ambrose repeatedly quoted the same biblical passage from Paul's Second Letter to the Corinthians: "The written law inflicts death whereas the spiritual law brings life." This scriptural quote seemed tailor-made for a man who dealt with the law every day in his role as a teacher. Ambrose saw that Augustine was approaching his personal problems in much the same manner that he dealt with the legal issues of his profession; trying to solve them logically with his head.

He elaborated on this core theme by further advising Augustine that he would not be able to find peace for his restless thoughts and feelings if he expected they would be dispelled by arguments similar to those found in legal manuals or some kind of concrete proofs that might stand up to scientific scrutiny. If you are seeking truths to live by, you have to take a leap beyond the confines of the rational world and engage not just your head but your whole person. If there were one key piece of advice that Ambrose was giving to Augustine, it might be summarized like this: "Stop being so legalistic and literal; trust the insights of your heart!"

This reminds me of an experience I had in my first year working as a clinical psychologist. A man came to see me for therapy who had just moved to town. After telling me the problems that brought him to the clinic, which dated back several years, I asked if he had previously sought help. He said yes, that he had recently seen someone but it turned out to be for only one session due to his unexpected move. He identified that therapist as none other than the well-known psychologist Dr. Rollo May.

Having spent my graduate years reading this man's books, I felt humbled to be following so closely in the footsteps of such a talented clinician. Recovering, I asked what I now think was a pretty good question: "Did you learn anything from him that might be helpful for us?" He replied that at the end of their session, Dr. May had made one remark that still stood out in his memory: "In my opinion, you think too much, and if we're going to make any progress that will have to change."

The advice given by Rollo May to my new client was essentially the same early counsel offered by Ambrose to Augustine. It is also similar to my opening suggestion to Charlie in his first session with me: Let's not try to "solve" your life as if it were a "problem." Helpful thoughts and feelings will emerge on their own if only you give yourself permission to loaf and invite your soul. During those times of retreat, explore your experiences with questions that go beyond whether they are right or wrong, logical or unreasonable. Approach your inner world in the same way that your high school English teacher advised you to read literature: with a willing suspension of judgment and disbelief.

Augustine learned how to do this himself and passed it on to us in the very first chapter of the *Confessions:* "Listen with the ears of your heart."

Augustine's relationship with Ambrose helped open up a whole new life within himself. It was not Ambrose's presence as a charismatic personality that brought about this change. Augustine's previous experiences with charismatic figures had left him wary of people who mainly seem to draw others to themselves as followers. The role of Ambrose in Augustine's life would be better described as catalytic. These individuals prompt others to look fruitfully at their own life. This is exactly what a sponsor does. Sponsors encourage us to pay attention to ourselves, not themselves. Ambrose functioned as Augustine's sponsor because he helped him to see and open up the treasure within himself.

Unfortunately, due to his busy schedule, Ambrose did not have the time to assist Augustine with the details of his self-discovery. He compensated for this by introducing him to the man who had served as his own personal "father," a link in the ancestral heritage of sponsorship that was now being passed on to yet another generation. "So I went to Simplicianus, the father of Ambrose." This introduction proved timely and the relationship turned out to be an excellent match.

Simplicianus took up right where Ambrose left off. Although well educated himself, he insisted from the outset that Augustine stop limiting his search for truth to his old academic habits of approaching problems solely with the intellect. He stressed the importance of learning from life itself by paying attention to his personal experiences. Simplicianus advised him that the truth and meaning he had been seeking since adolescence was right under his nose. It would become clearer if he took the time to examine the narrative of his own unique history.

Augustine applied this reflective approach across the whole range of his personal life. The *Confessions* shows how he paid close attention to his daily experiences, matching affect and events, in much the same ways that many people set out to do in modern psychotherapy. He also took a similar approach to scripture. He listened to his internal reactions as he slowly read the words of biblical passages. Simplicianus and Ambrose believed that scripture was a living document that spoke to each individual personally and that it was important to pay very careful attention to one's inner responses to the words. Directing his awareness to those internal reactions drew Augustine out of his head and allowed him to enter into the subjective realm of his soul.

Over the course of this time spent with Ambrose and Simplicianus, Augustine was also continuing to develop his personal and work life in Milan. He settled into the routine of teaching school. He reconciled with his mother and brought her, his now teenage son, and female companion to live with him and his friends in this new city. With the addition of his family and some new acquaintances, his small community was growing.

It was in the context of this more stable external framework and in the company of these caring relationships that Augustine made a decision that would change the course of this whole process. He resolved to stop a lifelong habit of passively enduring his soul's persistent restlessness and begin making more active efforts to recognize and understand what was going on in his inner life. He announced this decision in very practical terms: "I must plan my time and arrange my day for the good of my soul." This statement marked a major turning point in his life. It clearly delineated the moment of transition that we might now refer to as his "psychological conversion." This step turned out to be a prelude to a profound experience that would soon follow, one that would lead him to an awareness of the spiritual dimension of his life. Augustine shared this experience of his spiritual awakening in chapters seven and eight in his *Confessions*.

Augustine Describes
His Spiritual Awakening

On a day in September 386, Augustine was sitting in his home, quietly reading the Bible. He was trying to meditate on scripture as Ambrose and Simplicianus had taught him to do: with the eyes of his restless soul. As he gave more trust to his soul's perceptions that morning, he found himself having a new experience. The process of reading was slowly becoming less and less like an intellectual analysis and more like a kind of internal dialogue. He began to feel as if there were something alive within this ancient text that was reaching out to communicate with something alive at his own core. He decided to continue to trust his soul and further enter this experience through its eyes. He tells us that the first thing that he saw when he did this was a great light. "These books served to remind me to return to my own self. Under your guidance I entered into the depth of my soul, and this I was able to do because your depth befriended me. I entered, and with the eye of my soul, such as it was, I saw the light that never changes casting its rays over the same eye of my soul, over my mind."

What Augustine was seeing with the eyes of his soul was a glimpse into something that he himself could describe only as otherworldly. "What I saw was something quite, quite different from any light we know on earth. It shown above my mind, but not in the way that oil floats on water or the sky hangs over the earth. It was above me because it was itself the light that made me, and I was below because I was made by it. All who know the truth know this light, and all who know this light know eternity. It is the light that charity knows."

He then began to listen. What he heard with the ears of his soul revealed the identity of the light within him. The voice identified itself as being none other than the Author of Being and Light itself, the voice of God. "And far off, I heard your voice saying 'I am the God who Is.' I heard your voice as we hear voices that speak to our hearts, and at once I had no cause to doubt. I might more easily have doubted that I was alive than that truth had being. For we catch the sight of truth as he is known through his creation." Augustine was now seeing and hearing the truth that he had long sought. It was not a set of abstract ideas, but a living Being.

Furthermore, as he continued to listen, he heard this living Being express the desire to bridge the seemingly unfathomable gap between them and actually be joined with Augustine in a relationship. This was illustrated in the metaphor of a meal. Augustine experienced God offering to be the very food that he would eat. "I realized that I was far away from you. It was as though I were in a land where all is different from your own and I heard your voice calling from on high saying, 'I am the food of full grown men. Grow and you shall feed on me, but you shall not change me into your substance, as you do with the food of your body. Instead, you shall be changed into me.'"

For an instant, the veil of mystery was lifted. Augustine caught a glimpse of another land—a whole new dimension of experience that was so far away and yet so close. His first reaction was one of awe. "And so, in an instant of awe, my mind attained to the sight of the God who is."

Augustine experienced an immediate and overwhelming desire to accept the invitation and be joined with this God he had seen through the eyes of his soul. The prospect was so appealing that he did not want to do this for just this instant, however, but for the rest of his life. He had had a glimpse. He wanted his life to be transformed in whatever ways might be necessary so that he could live in that spiritual dimension and experience a continuing relationship with God.

Augustine seemed to grasp the distinction that is being made here between a psychological and a spiritual conversion. He summed it up in these words: "But you shall not change me into your substance, as you do with food for your body. Instead, you shall be changed into me." In his psychological conversion, Augustine had learned to listen to his soul and transform it into his bodily substance, that is, to discern his soul's guidance and try to incorporate what he learned into his daily life. Some twentieth-century psychologists, such as Abraham Maslow, have referred to this process as "self-actualization." In a spiritual conversion, however, Augustine could not change God into himself. Rather, he must allow himself to be taken into God. The process by which this could happen was profoundly confusing to him. He didn't know where to start.

The message of the vision was clear. If he chose this way, it would be God who would serve as the sponsor—the attentive presence at the threshold—offering the hand that would help him to cross over a boundary and enter into another realm. Even his soul must give up its authority and acknowledge God as the guide and ultimate source of truth. He would have to allow himself to be transformed by God, who would be both the initiator and the means. The whole process would be a gift that would come at God's timing and in God's way. This would require yet another acquiescence of pride and control, and a further step into blind trust. Augustine, who felt so accustomed to being in charge, felt helpless and confused. How was this transformation to happen?

Augustine Recounts His Spiritual Conversion

William James, in his well known classic, *The Varieties of Religious Experience,* speaks of "self-surrender" as a last step in the inner process of religious conversion. Once there has been an intuitive encounter with a Presence beyond oneself, the longing to change one's life in order to live in the gaze of that Presence can be overwhelming. Such a profound transformation, however, cannot be accomplished by sheer will. As James points out, the vital turning point of a spiritual conversion actually requires the exact opposite—relinquishment of will. In a spiritual conversion the individual must surrender his own personal authority to the Higher Power sensed by his soul.

Augustine described his experience of this surrender in terms that were consistent with the progression of his psychological awakening and conversion. In a psychological awakening, as we recall, the inner witness sensed the presence of what could be called the "soul" or the "self." In a spiritual awakening, it is the soul, in turn, that becomes aware of a Presence that exists even beyond itself. Augustine experienced this Presence as a loving "Being of Light," whom he called God.

His description of his spiritual conversion was also consistent with what he had gone through earlier on a psychological level. Psychological conversions are characterized by the inner witness forming a trusting relationship with the soul and coming to recognize it as a helpful guide. In a spiritual conversion, this same trusting relationship happens, but on another level. This time it is the soul that forms a trusting relationship with the Presence that it senses beyond itself. The soul makes such a great leap of trust that it surrenders its own autonomy and authority to this greater Being. This complete surrender, sometimes expressed in ecstatic terms, characterizes the last inner step in the process of a spiritual conversion. It is referred to many times in scriptures and is also summarized in a simple phrase that some Christians pray on a daily basis: "Thy will be done."

This profession of trusting surrender to a Divine Being is often expressed by the physical act of bowing or genuflecting. While living in the Islamic culture of my North African Peace

Corps village, I often witnessed the practice of deep bowing—prostration—that is part of that religious tradition. Catholics bow or genuflect when entering churches. Buddhists bow not only in temples but also in greeting, honoring the numinous Presence within each person. Augustine's next step in the process of his spiritual conversion will be marked externally by a defining act of deep prostration, which expresses his attitude of trusting surrender.

As the days and weeks passed after his initial vision, Augustine waited for something to happen. He was so ready for his life to be transformed, but he couldn't make it happen all by himself. He began to feel increasingly frustrated. Even in the span of this short period of time, he started to regress into his former habits. "In my weakness, I recoiled and fell back into my old ways, carrying within me nothing but the memory of something that I loved and longed for, as though I had sensed the fragrance of the fare but was not yet able to eat it."

He continued to visit with Ambrose and Simplicianus. They both encouraged him to persevere in his meditative readings of scripture. They shared with him their own experiences and those of others. These men provided more than support; they were down-to-earth examples of spiritual life in action. He looked up to them and they, as his sponsors, listened to him in ways that sustained his emerging soul. Augustine had found his path. In 386 he publicly acknowledged himself as a Christian. This acknowledgement came at a great price. The emperor Julian had passed a new law prohibiting Christians from teaching literature and rhetoric. He would lose his job and no longer practice his profession.

One day, when Augustine was at home expressing his frustration to his close friend Alypius, a fellow countryman from North Africa came to the door. While they were catching up on the news, the man noticed a copy of the Epistles of St. Paul lying on a table. He told Augustine and Alypius that he was a Christian and went on to elaborate in detail an emotional story of how the conversion of two of his friends had led him, in turn, to his own spiritual conversion.

Augustine was deeply affected by this personal confession. After the man left, he told Alypius that he felt he was being brought "face to face with myself." He was confronted once again with the same dilemma: "My inner self was a house divided against itself." He felt determined to do something right now to heal this painful split; he could no longer put it off.

The normally composed Augustine was overwhelmed by the powerful forces welling up inside of him. He rushed out the door into a garden attached to the house where they were living. Alypius ran after him and found his friend on a bench in a fetal position, tearing at his hair and hammering his forehead with his fists. He was chanting the same words over and over: "Let it be now! Let it be now!" He wanted to make a final leap into the abyss and trust that somehow this Presence would be there to receive him. "Cast yourself upon God and have no fear. He will not shrink away and let you fall. Cast yourself on him without fear, for he will welcome you and cure you of your ills." With this statement of faith, he cried out and "a great storm broke within me, bringing with it a great deluge of tears."

He then stood up and left Alypius. He ran farther into the garden, to a place where he might be totally alone. At the very center of that garden there was a fig tree. Augustine ran to this tree and flung himself beneath it sobbing. Lying on the ground, with his body heaving in spasms and tears, he offered himself to God. In an act of ultimate surrender, he turned over his whole life to God, completely and unconditionally. At that moment the old Augustine, in effect, expired. This was all that he could do. Whatever happened next would be the work of God, the free expression of God's compassion, the divine response that Christians call "grace."

When reading the *Confessions*, it is important to recognize when Augustine wanted us to understand what he wrote in metaphorical terms. This man, after all, was a teacher, steeped in the classical literature of his time. In this case, his audience would have been well aware of the symbolic importance of gardens throughout biblical references. Augustine could not have found a better image than a garden to describe his soul's encounter with God. Modern psychology also recognizes that our deepest experiences are essentially beyond words. That's why, when the soul "speaks," in dreams or profound spiritual experiences, it uses a language of images to convey what is linguistically inexpressible.

From that perspective, the first garden, the one located closest to the house, may have represented the inner world of Augustine's restless and tormented soul. This image recalls one of the rich meanings that Judeo-Christian literature has given to gardens. Although places of beauty, they also can be places of fear and suffering. In Eden and Gethsemani, for example, gardens provided the symbolic ground for transitions, where the human will encountered the divine. It was in those gardens where the ultimate question was raised: Will you follow your own will or the will of God? Traditionally, an affirmative reply was expressed by the Latin word *fiat*—"Let it be!" Augustine's response was wholehearted as he chanted "Let it be now! Let it be now!"

The second garden—the inner garden located even farther from the house—may have been Augustine's representation of a dimension even deeper within his soul. This was, for him, the place where he encountered the God of Life. The presence of God was portrayed by the tree of life, which grew in the very center of the garden.

Augustine threw himself at the base of that tree. This simple but powerful act of prostration at the feet of God was his way of conveying the defining moment of his spiritual conversion. It was an act of trusting submission that represented the complete and unconditional sacrifice of his own will to the will of God. This pledge of total surrender allowed his soul to pass over into the realm of the spirit and enter the sacred feast. It was here that he experienced the nourishing renewal of his life that filled him with divine light and brought a sense of peace so deep that it calmed his restless heart: "(I)t was as though the light of confidence flooded into my heart and all the darkness of doubt dispelled."

In 1966, an American monk named Thomas Merton wrote a simple but profound line in his poem "All the Way Down" that expressed his own experience of what Augustine also must have encountered some 1600 years earlier: "I've seen the room where life and death are made."

Eight

Passing It On: The Challenge of Our Middle Years

It is not surprising that both Charlie and Augustine would make some changes in their day-to-day lives after these inner transformations. It also is not unusual that such changes would take place when they did. The forties and fifties are a period of time when many men make minor and even major adjustments in their work and love relationships. At middle age, enough years have passed to see the consequences of taking one direction and sufficient time remains to merit some correction of the course. Those who decide to modify their lives can relate to Dante's description of this process as he expressed it in the opening lines of his *Divine Comedy:* "In the middle of the journey of our life I came to my senses in a dark forest, for I had lost the straight path."

From a developmental standpoint, the "middle of the journey" also comes at a time when there is an intersection between advanced social development and higher levels of psychological awareness. Erikson outlined the progression of healthy social development from adolescent identity formation ("Who am I to be?") to the activation challenges of young adulthood ("How do I implement my identity?"), and then on to true adult life ("Where is my place in maintaining the world as a member of the generation in charge?"). He showed us how each level builds on the previous one in successive steps. Carl Rogers similarly outlined the development of psychological awareness in a series of stages that demonstrate how the soul lies at the center of this process.

At midlife, we find ourselves at the intersection of these two developmental sequences. Social commitments of love and work have begun to take on a more manageable routine, leaving time to pause, draw a breath, and perhaps even invite the soul. Whether such introspection is fostered by leisure or provoked by tragedy, middle age is a prime time for men to scrutinize the extent to which their soul's preferences are actually being lived out in the commitments they've made in love and work. This intersection of advanced social development and increased psychological awareness is an essential ingredient that is specifically characteristic of midlife reflection.

Another key element is consciousness of time. You can tell when you are thinking like a middle-aged man when you start reflecting on your life more in terms of time remaining and less in terms of time past. Some men experience a clear awareness of death itself. Consequently, if you also feel, as Dante described, that you have "lost the straight path," you will probably experience an added urgency to any desire for change.

Augustine's illness in Rome provided his first real encounter with death and brought up serious questions about where his life was headed. Charlie's loss of his father, his marriage, and family, as well as his relationship with Susan, led him into therapy where he found himself facing time constraints if he had any hope of salvaging his adolescent hunches of who he was to be. In his own unique way, each of these men was facing what contemporary psychologists would refer to as a midlife transition.

When men slow down and invite their souls during these middle years, some become less interested in totaling up the score and more inclined to start viewing their life as a journey with precious time remaining. They may acknowledge for the first time the wrongs they have done to others and themselves. As they learn to match outer events with inner reactions they repeat a process that was essential to their adolescent identity formation and now clarifies similar choices that are being revisited in the present. The seeming chaos of the inner world can gradually take on some predictability and integrity. Feelings, dreams, and fantasies become recognized as the persistent and consistent voice of the soul. When these men see the helpfulness of their soul's perceptions, they may start to trust them. This leads many to recognize discrepancies between their inner sense of identity and the outer reality of their day-to-day lives. The distress of having "lost the straight path" prompts some to seek change.

Carl Jung said that it is the persona that usually changes last. *Persona* is the Greek word for "mask," and Jung used this term to describe the outer "face" that we present to the world. It is often seen in little things, like the clothes we wear and what we drive, but is also present in the larger "face" of our public role and the level of attachment we have to it.

We all need a persona in order to function in the social world, but there is a danger when it separates us from our true identity. Problems occur if we become overattached to this public function ("I am a psychologist," or teacher, or priest, and so on). Overidentification, even to an accurate role persona, still alienates us from ourselves. There also can be problems if our outer persona is an inadequate match for our inner identity. In either case, anyone getting more in touch with his soul's perceptions may find himself taking his public "face" a little less seriously. Or he may want to change some of its details to give himself more room to express the person he really is. That is why we may find ourselves—or our friends at midlife—making some modifications to our person or possessions. We are bringing our outer persona into straighter alignment with our inner identity.

Some men jokingly refer to these changes as reliving their adolescence. This insight has more than a grain of truth to it.

Whether midlife changes are forged in the complexities of work and love relationships or carried out simply in the way we dress or drive, they have a lot in common with those earlier phases of development when we were trying to understand who we truly were inside and how to make those preferences happen in the outer world. This time around, however, we have the hindsight to see what worked and what didn't and the time to make some corrections. Whatever we are considering is important.

Charlie saw how he had become overidentified with his functional role of being a grocer. By tailoring his personal life to fit this one social identity, he neglected his family commitments as well as himself. He had not followed through on his dreams of being a teacher, nor been faithful to the visions of marriage and family that he and Joyce had forged together back when they were dating. His heart filled with sadness for how much time had been lost creating a life that fit him so poorly in both work and love. It was this grief that ushered him into the desire to alter his life in whatever ways might still be possible. The point of these intended changes was not to be more "successful" or even a "better person." Charlie simply wanted to become more of Charlie, the person he sensed himself to be.

He focused first on his work and he started cautiously. Charlie signed up to be a volunteer teacher of basic English-speaking skills to newly arrived immigrants from Southeast Asia. The preparation for doing this kind of teaching required that he attend six two-hour sessions that met on Saturday mornings. He specialized in learning classroom teaching methods rather than individual tutorials because he remembered how much he had enjoyed his practice teaching in college. After completing the training, Charlie agreed to teach a one-hour class two times a week to a group that usually numbered about twelve students.

By delegating some of his duties at the store and applying this time to teaching, Charlie felt more energy and vitality than he had in years. He spent hours preparing his lesson plans, jokingly described his teaching style as "more enthusiastic than skillful," and stayed after class to talk with anyone who needed help. It was a perfect fit. Charlie felt like he had "come home." He saw students come alive in his classes and shared their excitement as they tried out new words at work. He specialized in teaching vocabulary connected with grocery products. When the semester ended, he signed up for a second one without any hesitation.

Charlie was beginning to feel less "stuck" and "trapped" in his old routines. As so often happens, when you truly loosen up one part of your life, you find yourself freeing up a whole lot more. He became a more active father to his two boys. Not just as a "Disney dad" (those separated fathers who show up mainly for the splashy events), but on a more daily basis. "If I do say so myself, I'm a whole lot more fun to be with," he explained when I asked about what was prompting this big shift. Indeed, he was. Charlie wasn't ready to resume dating yet, but was looking into a computer matching service recommended by a friend. He also joined a coffee group of men from his parish who met on Saturday mornings at McDonald's to share their lives and talk about the scripture readings for the upcoming Sunday Mass.

I haven't seen Charlie in several years. When we last talked, he asked me for a referral to a spiritual director. I gave him the names of two nuns from a local Benedictine monastery who were trained in this specialized ministry. I don't know if he went on to pursue the further education he would need to become a certified teacher, or if he is dating, or went to see a spiritual advisor. I do know that Charlie is a born teacher and is surely continuing to do something in that field. I know that he has set his feet on a course of fatherhood that will never stop. I am also confident that he is ready to date again and that the next relationship has a better chance. I know that he will be in good hands if he follows up on either one of those referral names.

The main basis for my optimism is that I have seen Charlie's psychological conversion. He is on the "straight path" and won't go back. Like Augustine, he now plans his time and arranges his day for the good of his soul. Everyone who touches Charlie will benefit from his presence.

Augustine told us in the *Confessions* about the conversion of life that he made following his experience in the garden in 386. It involved a number of very large changes over a period of about ten years. The first thing he did was to give up the promising academic position that he had dedicated so many years to attain. He ended a formal engagement to be married. He uprooted his well-established and comfortable life in Milan and moved back to his hometown in North Africa. He became an active member of his church and was eventually ordained a priest.

While he was in the midst of making all these changes, most of the important people in his life died. He lost his mother, his only son, one of his oldest and dearest friends, and his sponsor Ambrose. Filled with grief for all these losses as well as the years he wasted before his conversion, Augustine described his emotional state at the time he wrote the *Confessions* as one of "broken bones." It was Camus who said, "I entered literature through worship." Augustine may well have entered literature through grief.

As he wrote the *Confessions* in 397, he was a forty-three-year-old man on the brink of an important transition in his life. He was about to become a bishop. It was a position he had neither sought nor desired but felt obliged to accept. At the very least, he wanted his service as a church administrator to embody the vitality of his spiritual conversion and not degenerate into just another exercise of bureaucratic functionality.

Augustine never considered his conversion to be complete. As if to illustrate this, the *Confessions* did not end with the story of his spiritual transformation, or even his subsequent baptism. He added four more chapters, each of which depict a man struggling to remember that his soul was rooted in God while he endured daily storms of distraction, poor health, and temptations. Even as he wrote the later chapters, he was still citing a detailed litany of his continuing conflicts with sex, greed, and a form of excessive self-care that he referred to as "self-complacency." The postconversion Augustine did not provide us with any images of a confident man who finally felt strong in the sense of being less vulnerable.

He accepted vulnerability as a natural part of life, understanding this to be true not only for himself but also for those in his care. Augustine's ideal of psychological and spiritual well-being was not defined in terms of a fixed state that could be reached once and for all. Psycho-spiritual health was precarious and needed to be sustained by daily attention to the soul in meditation and prayer. He continued to plan his time and arrange his day for the good of his soul. He discarded any dualistic notions about being either a sinner or a saint. In his life of service as a bishop, he strived for sanctity while being deeply conscious of his faults.

A Life of Generativity Provides Meaning during the Middle Years

The midlife changes made by Charlie and Augustine were not primarily motivated by a wish to become more successful. Rather, they were rooted in a deep need to carry out their individual adult choices for maintaining the world in ways that felt more alive and meaningful. Each visible change expressed a desire for a life filled with increased vitality and purpose.

One fundamental benefit of taking on the work associated with being an adult is that some of the tasks involved provide us with an opportunity for experiencing what psychologists refer to as "efficacy"—that satisfying sense of being productive and effective. Unfortunately, the path to efficacy is too often strewn with so many tasks and duties that there is little space left over for the soul. A typical response to the question "How are you?" becomes "Busy!" Daily life has been taken over by a kind of function lust, and satisfaction declines.

The imbalance between external participation and internal reflection eventually leads to a reduction of meaning and vitality. When middle-aged men describe this condition, they use words such as *stuck, restless, trapped, emotionally disconnected,* or even *burned out.* Erik Erikson gave a name to the phenomenon of being too caught up in one's busy routine to have time for oneself. He called it "stagnation."

Stagnation is a catch-all term that expresses that dull but persistent pain some adult men feel when they are being reminded of the presence of their neglected soul. Augustine felt it in the form of chronic restlessness. Charlie endured nagging feelings of dissatisfaction, problems sleeping, and persistent fatigue. At the source of each man's unique stagnation was his soul's healthy desire to be recognized and participate in his adult responsibilities of maintaining the world. Only the soul can infuse love and work with vitality and meaning.

Erikson also had a word for the healthy exercise of midlife productivity. He called it "generativity." Generativity begins with the inclusion of the soul in the day-to-day responsibilities of living. The etymological roots of this word are meaningfully connected to one of man's deepest biopsychological drives: the desire to bring forth and sustain life. That's what midlife generativity is all about.

In his book *Childhood and Society,* Erikson defined the essential quality of generativity as "primarily the concern in establishing and guiding the next generation." He went on to say that this responsibility extends even beyond the regard for our own offspring, and has to do with the enhancement of life for anyone in our care. Ironically, psycho-spiritual development from here on out depends on the extent to which we also establish and guide people other than ourselves. The primary developmental challenge of midlife is to transcend our own needs. Erikson later referred to generativity as the "central" developmental task for all of adult life.

What Erikson referred to as "generativity" lies at the very heart of what is meant here by "sponsorship." Both generativity and sponsorship are concerned with more than the functional skill enhancement and socialization that we adults provide to the next generation as their parents, teachers, and mentors. Generativity and sponsorship are directed at the soul—bringing the soul to life. Just as each of us grew and developed in the gaze of significant others, so now our continued development requires that we provide that same enlivening gaze to the next generation. The central task of midlife psycho-spiritual development is to maintain the world as a sponsor.

The act of writing the *Confessions* was a therapeutic process for Augustine. This exercise prepared him to be a bishop by forging a bridge between his role as a church leader and the enlivening presence of his soul. He readied himself to take on these new duties by calling forth the memories of all those who had sponsored his own life. As a bishop, he wanted his words to touch others, as those of Ambrose and Simplicianus had moved him. He prayed that he might carry out his duties with compassion, as he remembered the patience and kindness of his mother. He wrote to remind himself of all the friends who had supported his inner journey, so that he might support others, as they responded to the confusing process emerging from within their own souls. He wanted the spiritual heritage of God's sponsorship to flow through the work of his hands and generate life in each part of the world he touched.

The changes made by Charlie also reflected this same healthy midlife transition. His new work as a teacher rose from similar deep roots, bringing a continuity between his soul and his outer life, and thus generating vitality in others. As a person who was genuinely being himself, he became sincerely interested in the selves of others. His presence enlivened receptive students and enriched their lives in ways that went beyond increased competency in the subject matter. Charlie's newfound sense of vitality and purpose could be felt by all of us, and it was catching. His sons looked forward to seeing him; they'd finally found the man who was their father.

When a man discovers the "straight path" of his soul and allows it to flow into his outer activities, the external changes he makes may not be as dramatic as those carried out by Augustine. We are more likely to encounter people like Charlie. What we notice is simply that this person seems more alive in himself and more interested in the life of the world around him. This is what Erikson meant by midlife "generativity." We can't understand it simply by looking at changes in external behavior, no matter how large or small. The changes essential to this developmental period truly come from within. If we want to understand what is going on in healthy psycho-spiritual development at midlife, we have to direct our primary attention to the inner life. As Thomas Merton wrote during his own middle years in *My Argument with the Gestapo:* "If you want to know who I am, do not ask me what I eat, where I live or how I part my hair. Ask me what I live for and ask me in detail."

Nine

Sustaining a Sense of Integrity during the Later Part of Life

As a graduate student in psychology, I specialized in gerontology and spent several years doing research for my dissertation on the topic of retirement. When I started out, in the late 1960s, the opportunity to plan a postwork life was a fairly recent social phenomenon. The financial freedom provided by Social Security and pensions, along with medical advances that increased longevity, offered men additional years and the means to pursue new interests. Retirement itself had become a developmental marker that signaled the opening of a different phase of life with its own unique set of challenges and opportunities.

My particular interest in this vast field had to do with understanding what factors promoted healthy psychological development in the lives of retired men. My hypothesis was that we needed the same context for psychological growth in later life that had been necessary for previous developmental transitions. If we were born hardwired to connect and it was in the context of these relationships that earlier stages of development took place, why should it be different in the later years?

Not everyone agreed with this. One theory about later adult psycho-social development, called "disengagement theory," held exactly the opposite. According to disengagement theory, in the normal course of later life, the individual and society mutually withdraw from each other. As people relinquish roles they played during their adult years, their social circle narrows. Disengagement theory proposed that these gradual disconnections were not only the expected course of events, but also helpful later on because they provided the individual with time to review his life as he prepared for the ultimate disengagement, which is death.

My own research focused on the three-year period immediately following retirement. I was interested in the level of satisfaction reported by these recently retired men who were experiencing good health, sufficient income, and a spouse who was still alive and well. You would expect that this would be the group most likely to report high satisfaction, and they did. However, what about the ones who met all of the above criteria and still described themselves as dissatisfied? Did these men have anything in common that set them apart?

The results of my study suggested that the main factor associated with dissatisfaction among retirees in this optimal group (healthy, financially secure, and living with a spouse) was their feeling that they were socially isolated. The men who reported the most unhappiness with their lives were the ones whose social involvements were insufficient to connect them with the wider community. In other words, it was continued social engagement, not disengagement, that promoted well-being in men going through the period immediately following retirement.

There are two stages in this postretirement process. The first phase takes place immediately following departure from work, which was the time focus of my research. The second phase begins about three years after retirement. We benefit from engagement with the community during both of these stages, but in different ways and for different reasons.

The first stage is usually quite active. It is an initial period of adjustment that lasts for about three years. During this transition time, most men are trying out various activities in leisure, travel, volunteering, part-time employment, or even continued work in the same or a whole new field. If this experimentation leads to discovering enjoyable and meaningful new pursuits, a comfortable rhythm is found, anxiety lessens, and increased satisfaction is reported. The transition phase is then essentially complete.

From a developmental perspective, this transitional period has some things in common with the early adult phase. When we relinquish our functional role in the mainstream of the community, we can expect to encounter some of the same questions about love and work that we faced as we entered it in our early twenties. What can we do to promote a feeling of efficacy and usefulness in the community? How can we make social connections that will sustain our sense of identity and belonging?

Once again, we make this transition with our feet, through trial and error. It requires patience from the person going through it and support from the family and friends watching it unfold. The good news is that after this transitional period is settled and a sense of balance reestablished, most men actually report improvements in their health and happiness.

Just as we needed sponsoring connections within the community to establish our original place in the adult world, so now we need those same vital relationships as we reestablish ourselves in the postwork world. Normalizing disengagement may inadvertently endorse the kind of ageist stereotypes that too long have marginalized older adults once they left the workforce. We should not presume that dropping roles reflects a wish to be less involved. Many retired men want to continue giving to the community in some way and need the opportunities to do so. The supportive connections provided by sponsors are important not only for this transitional period, but also for the next stage of development.

After a comfortable postretirement rhythm is reestablished, a second developmental process begins to emerge out of the stability. This next stage is less visible and manifests itself in more subtle forms. It is characterized by a renewed interest in one's past and evidenced in the recall of earlier life events, which may be shared through stories. Even though this healthy process has a more inner focus, relationships with others are no less important for it to thrive. Current connections in the community as well as those that were established in the past are both key to the unfolding of this next phase of psycho-spiritual growth.

Maintaining Integrity: The Challenge of Our Later Years

Erik Erikson referred to the developmental process associated with late adulthood as the time to "ripen the fruit." In chapter seven of *Childhood and Society,* he linked this stage to the previous ones through his basic theme of generativity. "Only in him who in some way has taken care of things and people and has adapted himself to the triumphs and disappointments adherent to being the originator of others or the generator of products and ideas—only in him gradually ripen the fruit of these seven stages." This ripening is described as both "hard to define" and "dearly paid for." It grows out of a basic proclivity for finding some sense of meaning for our lives. Ultimately, it is fostered by a desire to face our death with an assurance that we have lived our life with some measure of integrity.

The maturing and ripening associated with later adult development is not a passive process. It requires an active nurturing through honest reflection. Just as Erikson used terms like *maintenance of the world* to describe the challenges faced in adult development, he chose equally vivid words to define the tasks associated with late adult development. He called for the creation of a "world order." Erikson advised us to do no less than review our past history with an eye to creating a coherent narrative designed to give a sense of meaning and order to our life. "It is the acceptance that one's one-and-only life cycle was something that had to be and that, by necessity, permitted of no substitutions...." Erikson explicitly recognized that the task of creating order out of seeming randomness had both psychological and spiritual significance.

People undertake this process in a variety of ways. I know someone who helps older adults shape a formal narrative out of their life history. She uses a loosely structured interview, listens to the emerging experiences, and then helps that person organize these past events into coherent stories that come to resemble a biography. The finished product becomes a meaningful record that also can be passed on to family and friends. Others prefer to sort out their past through the creation of documents such as letters, journals, scrapbooks, or photo albums. Some engage in prayerful reflection on their lives, either alone or in a like-minded group. Still others talk out their stories in dialogues with a trusted friend, spiritual director, or therapist. The ones that I see in psychotherapy initially may come in with a pressing problem. Once that is resolved, some stay on to make a more extensive review of their past.

One client of mine, a seventy-eight-year-old retired businessman named John, originally sought help after a diagnosis of lung cancer, which is now in remission. He has remained in therapy because the medical incident prompted him to take a more comprehensive look at his life. During a recent session, he told me about a daily spiritual practice that he has maintained for many years. He said that he starts each day with about ten minutes of prayer. He begins with a salutation: "All honor to God, the Giver of Life." He then reads one psalm and spends a few minutes reflecting on whatever word or phrase catches his attention. At the conclusion of his meditation, John calls to memory the names and visual images of eleven people whom he remembers as standing out over the years for their care and support. He slowly brings to mind the faces of his father, his daughter, his oldest friend, his wife, a priest whom he met in high school, two current friends, and several others. Four of these people died years ago and some others he hasn't seen for a long time.

This daily exercise illustrates the inner role of sponsors in private self-reflection. John begins by placing himself in the presence of God, explicitly acknowledging the ultimate origins of his life. He then meditates on one of the psalms as a way of tuning his soul to God's presence. Finally, he seeks to reconnect himself to the vitality he has sustained over the years by recalling the gaze of the people who welcomed his soul into the world. Even though some of them are absent, they each continue to function as a viable part of the community that supports him. Inviting them back into his heart once again allows him to summon up their strength and care as he sets out to face another day.

John is a good example of our increasing reliance on inner resources as we age and lose the functional roles and important relationships that previously served as our supports. The community that sustains us in later adulthood is a mixture of people who are both external and internal, present and past. Whether we are seeking the strength to face another day or setting out, as Erikson advised, on a more thorough review of our life, it helps to recognize that even in the face of deep losses we still are not completely alone. Our vitality and honesty are enhanced when we acknowledge the ultimate origins of our life and recognize our continued dependence on the community that sponsored it, whether its members are present in person or in memory.

The identification of sponsors also is one of the best places to start for anyone trying to create some world order out of a seemingly chaotic life. Who were the people whose presence brought me to life and welcomed me into the community beyond myself?

These were and are my "parents"—the "mothers" and "fathers" who were there in the beginnings and remain with me in some form to this day. They deserve gratitude and, if there are fences to be mended, efforts toward reconciliation.

Productive self-reflection takes place in the gaze of these compassionate witnesses, who call to mind the original sources of the truth-seeking witness—not the critic—within ourselves. They also will be the focal points around whom we can begin organizing our past experiences. As we bring them to our attention, the events and feelings associated with their presence will emerge. These are the memories that evoke the origins of our vitality. They can be shaped into stories that chronicle the progressive development of our life.

We ourselves can serve, in turn, as sponsors to other people engaged in this developmental process. We do this by actively encouraging them to tell us about their lives, and then reflectively listening to the stories that emerge. Sometimes posing questions helps stimulate memories or draws out meanings latent within the narratives. Another older client shared with me a list of questions that someone had given him to take along on an upcoming retreat. Whom have you loved in your life? What experiences have you cherished? What ideas brought you liberation? What are the convictions you lived for? What are the insights you have gained into God, the world, human nature, love, religion, prayer? What are the risks that you took? The sufferings that seasoned you? Who are the people who shaped your life? The events? Which scripture texts lit your path? What are your achievements? Your regrets and unfulfilled desires? Who are the persons enshrined in your heart?

When you look at these questions, they don't call forth answers but stimulate what is, hopefully, a familiar style of self-inquiry. The purpose of this kind of reflection, however, is different for older adults. During middle age, life was usually examined for the purpose of solving immediate problems or

adjusting the course of love and work commitments to better follow the soul's guidance. Older adults are more likely to explore
their past history to settle accounts and find more ultimate meanings. Erikson said that, as we age, our self-reflection becomes
more focused on how well we have "taken care of things and
people...." Our sense of self-esteem will hinge on how we are
able to respond to that question.

In the end, the identification of our sponsors and the questions about our past that we ponder in their gaze probably won't
lead to a simple assessment of how much money we made or
power we achieved. The truly ultimate questions about our maintenance of the world are far more basic than issues of monetary
accumulation or functional accomplishment. They lead us to the
very roots of our psychological and spiritual lineage. These questions have to do with people and finding a sense of meaning for
our life that only the soul can provide. How well have I endowed
the next generation with the life-affirming heritage I received
from those who sponsored me? To what extent have I passed on
the life I received? In Erikson's terms, have I been generative?

Generativity—the care for life in ourselves and others—is the
outward sign of healthy psychological development and of true
spiritual maturity. Sponsorship is the active expression of this
generative energy. The very act of being a sponsor advances the
process of growth in both the giver and the receiver. Sponsorship
is the way that men express their innate desire to bring forth and
sustain life.

The creative Source of this generative life can be found in the
depths of the soul. The soul is the place where psychology and
spirituality find common ground. Augustine believed that if we
listen carefully, we will hear its primal restlessness. The soul is
restless, he said, until it rests in God. It is so fundamentally
rooted in the Ground of Being that any apparent distinctions
between psychological and spiritual life eventually become artifi-

cial and irrelevant. The presence that we express and touch in our efforts to sponsor life in others is, ultimately, the compassionate Presence that enlivens each soul. The guidance and meaning that we seek to sustain a life of purpose and hope rises, ultimately, from the Truth that unfolds in the depths of our soul. One spiritual writer, a Spanish monk named John of the Cross, wrote about the complete trust he placed in his soul to see and follow the Light that guided the path of his own spiritual journey: "I went without discerning and with no other Light than that which in my heart was burning."

Let this also be true for each of us, and may we honor that life by planning our time and arranging each day for the good of our souls.

Annotated Bibliography

(The following books are among those cited and used in the text.)

Augustine. The *Confessions*. Translated by R. S. Coffin. Baltimore: Penguin Books, 1961. (This is the same edition I first read and is quoted here.)

Buber, Martin. *I and Thou*. Translated by Ronald Smith. New York: Charles Scribner's Sons, 1958. (This is an eloquent statement of the common ground occupied by psychology and religion.)

Erikson, Erik. *Childhood and Society*. New York: Norton & Company, 1963. (This classic text on development is the framework for my ideas.)

Erikson, Erik. *Insight and Responsibility*. New York: Norton & Company, 1964. (Kathleen Stewart's footnote on p. 198 guided my professional life.)

James, William. *The Varieties of Religious Experience*. New York: New American Library, 1958. (This is the 1902 classic on psychology and religion.)

Menninger, Karl. *Whatever Became of Sin?* New York: Bantam Books, 1979. (The conscience is described in psychological and religious terms.)

Merton, Thomas. *My Argument with the Gestapo*. Garden City, NY: Doubleday, 1969. (Merton bridges the psychological and spiritual worlds.)

Merton, Thomas. *The Collected Poems of Thomas Merton.* New York: New Directions, 1977. (This is an excellent anthology of his inspiring verse.)

Rilke, Rainer Maria. *Selected Poems.* Translated by Robert Bly. New York: Harper & Row, 1981. (His poetry describes the struggle for psycho-spiritual authenticity.)

Rogers, Carl. *On Becoming a Person.* Boston: Houghton Mifflin, 1961. (His stages of psychological awareness are outlined in chapter 7.)

Tillich, Paul. *Dynamics of Faith.* New York: Harper Torchbooks, 1957. (Tillich writes in terms compatible with psychology and theology.)